MW00474374

Southern Holiday Feast

Thanksgiving, Christmas, New Year's, Easter & More!

S. L. Watson

Copyright © 2015 S. L. Watson

All rights reserved.

ISBN: 9781549984358

All rights reserved. No part of this book may be reproduced or utilized in any form or by any means, electronic or mechanical, including photocopying and recording without express written permission from the author and/or copyright holder. This book is for informational or entertainment purposes only. Cover design S. L. Watson 2015. Picture courtesy of Canva.

The author has made every effort to ensure the information provided in this book is correct. Failure to follow directions could result in a failed recipe. The author does not assume and hereby disclaim any liability to any party for any loss, damage, illness or disruption caused by errors and omissions, whether such errors and omissions result from negligence, accident or any other cause.

The author has made every effort to provide accurate information in the creation of this book. The author accepts no responsibility and gives no warranty for any damages or loss of any kind that might be incurred by the reader or user due to actions resulting from the use of the information in this book.

The user assumes complete responsibility for the use of the information in this book.

DEDICATION

To my wonderful family for all the glorious memories created through the years!

CONTENTS

INTRODUCTION

In the South, food plays a major role in holiday gatherings. From Thanksgiving, Christmas, New Year's, Brunch, Memorial Day, July 4th, Labor Day and parties, you will find a wide variety of recipes for your holiday table or barbecue.

Turkey, ham, goose, duck, appetizers, breads, pies, cakes, candies, stuffing recipes, cookies, side dishes and even leftover recipes are all included. I've included menu ideas to help you plan the perfect feast.

My mother made every holiday a special occasion. She would have a spread on the table you would not believe. It wasn't fancy food but just great Southern cooking. Christmas was especially important to my mother. No matter where you lived, you had to come home for Christmas. We had a large family but mother prepared a feast for everyone.

Christmas was not about presents. We always had homemade gifts but she made the whole month of December special. In our house, Christmas was about family. The whole family would be together for a wonderful time.

Mother had several traditions for the holidays. On the first Saturday of December, all the women would gather to make candy for the holidays. It was one of my favorite traditions growing up. The house would smell of chocolate, fresh caramel cooking on the stove and all the women sharing their new versions of traditional candy recipes. To this day, I still make my holiday candies on the first Saturday in December. There would be potato candy, caramels, chocolate covered cherries, pralines, fudge and numerous other candies.

On the 3rd Saturday in December, it was cookie baking time. The spell of vanilla extract and sugar would just make your mouth water. Of course, I could never wait for the cookies to cool so we could decorate them. Though my mother has now gone to be with the Lord, we still follow her traditions.

The holidays are about family and food. It is not about expensive gifts. We had gifts and I still cherish those homemade gifts more than anything. I prefer a food gift to anything else. The love that goes into homemade gifts make them all the more treasured. The greatest holidays in my memory, were spent with my family enjoying the fruits of our labor.

HOLIDAY MENU SUGGESTIONS

Thanksgiving Dinner Menu

Appetizers & Beverages

Southern Sausage Balls
Mama's Cheese Ball with crackers
Vegetable & Fruit Tray
Cranberry Punch

Dinner

Roast Turkey
Maple Pecan Glaze Baked Ham
Southern Cornbread Dressing
Cranberry Pecan Stuffing
Giblet Gravy
Turkey Pan Drippings Gravy
Marshmallow Whipped Sweet Potatoes
Mashed Potatoes
Green Bean Casserole
Lemon Green Beans
Deviled Eggs
Macaroni & Cheese
Mama's Squash Casserole
Maple Apple Carrots
Cranberry Sauce
Perfect Sunday Dinner Rolls
Pecan Pie
Chocolate Pecan Pie
Southern Chess Pie
Sweet Potato Pie
Pumpkin Pie
Brandied Apple Walnut Cake

Christmas Brunch Menu

Texas Game Hens
Apple Brunch Strata
Pecan Waffles
Buttery Vanilla Breakfast Scones
Sausage and Bacon
Easy Sausage Mini Muffins
Parmesan Omelet with Cheddar Sauce
Honey Fruit Salad
Cherry Pineapple Cups
Melon Mango Juice
Blueberry Apple Juice Blast

Christmas Dinner Menu

Appetizers & Beverages

Toasted Baguette Slices with Peach Salsa
Shrimp Salsa with tortilla chips
Southern Salted Pecans
Trader's Punch
Mother's Famous Sugar Cookies
Me Maw's Divinity
Potato Candy

Dinner

Spicy Prime Rib
Fruited Roast Duck
Sausage Cornbread Stuffing
Lemon Herb Stuffing
Perfect Sunday Dinner Rolls
Vegetable Casserole
Artichoke Salad
Maple Syrup Sweet Potatoes
Orange Baby Carrots
Basil Tomatoes
Cooked green beans
Brussel Sprouts with Bacon
Spinach Au Gratin
Coconut Cake
Southern Red Velvet Cake
Lemon Chess Pie
Coconut Cream Pie
Chocolate Pie
Pecan Tassies

Holiday Party Menu

Appetizers & Beverages

Brisket BBQ Poppers
Bacon Wands
Cumin Guacamole Dip
Pecan Cheese Log with crackers
Fruit & cheese platter
Whiskey Sour Punch
Red Roosters
Trader's Punch

Main Dish Items

Holiday Glazed Ham
Italian Baked Shrimp
Coca Cola Beef Brisket
Tangerine Rice
Scalloped Green Beans
Sage Dinner Braid

Desserts

Choose A Flavor Tassies
Chocolate Caramel Fudge
Kentucky Colonels
Bourbon Balls
German Chocolate Cake
Strawberry Christmas Candies

New Year's Eve Party

Appetizers & Beverages

Shrimp with Herb Jalapeno Cheese
Easy Onion Beef Triangles
Crisp Cheddar Cubes
Sugar Roasted Almonds
Crispy Baked Buffalo Shrimp
Corn Fritters with Cilantro Cream Sauce
Baked Santa Fe Dip
Champagne Peach Punch
Orange Mint Juleps
Tea Berry Sangria

Main Dish Items

Pineapple Roast Duck
Herb Marinated Salmon
Grilled Beef Tenderloin with Mushrooms
Herb Cheese Pull Apart Rolls

Desserts

Old Fashioned Millionaires
Chocolate Brittle
Southern Pralines
Southern Caramel Cake
Brown Sugar Peach Pie
Pineapple Chess Pie

New Year's Day Menu
Appetizers

Bacon Wands
Sausage Mushrooms
Marinated Meatballs
Bacon Pepper Jack Chicken Wings

Main Dish Items
Hoppin' John
Dixie Pork & Sweets
Turnip Greens with Bacon
Sweet Potato Balls
Flank Steak Pinwheels
Purple Hull Peas

New Year's Day Brunch

Homemade Biscuits
Sausage, Bacon and Ham
Southern Waffles
Spinach Mushroom Breakfast Casserole
Island Pancakes
Three Cheese Quiche
Fruit Platter
Orange and Strawberry Cream
Ribbon Cheese Loaf
Shrimp Salsa
Blackberry Dumplings
Apple Cinnamon Rolls

Easter Brunch Menu

Overnight Veggie Sausage Strata
Sausage, Bacon & Ham
Orange Bow Knots
Pear Almond Quesadillas
Apple Pancakes with Cider Sauce
Miniature Lemon Sugar Loaves
Puff Pancake with Summer Berries
Sweetened Grapes
Southern Stuffed Ham
Miniature Frosted Coconut Cupcakes
Fresh Fruit Platter
Assorted Cheese Platter
Minted Melon Balls

Easter Dinner Menu

Appetizers

Marinated Shrimp
Caramel Nut Corn
Toasted Baguette Slices with Peach Salsa
Fruit & Cheese Platter

Dinner

Roast Goose with Stewed Apples
Pineapple Glazed Ham
Southern Cornbread Dressing
Orange Dressing
Fresh Green Beans
Corn Custard Casserole
Coconut Sweet Potato Bake
Tangerine Rice
Deviled Eggs
Maple Apple Carrots
Fruit Filled Acorn Squash
Sour Cream Potato Salad
Mushroom Scalloped Potatoes
Onion Biscuits

Desserts

Coconut Cake
Carrot Cake
Peanut Butter Easter Eggs
Coconut Cream Pie
Marshmallow Coconut Pie

Memorial Day BBQ Menu

Satan's Wings
Southern Barbecue Shrimp
Coca Cola Beef Brisket
Summer Garden Potato Salad
Deviled Eggs
Easy Baked Beans
Garden Row Salad
Grilled Corn
Glazed Apple Brownies
Blackberry Apple Pie
Lemon Creme Parfaits
Herb Cheese Pull Apart Rolls

July 4th Party Menu

Coca Cola Beef Brisket
Grilled Georgia Peach Barbecue Chicken
Grilled Mushroom Burgers
Southern Cole Slaw
Artichoke Salad
Grilled Cantaloupe Wedges
Summer Fruit Bowl
Stardust Salad
Assorted fresh vegetables
Onion Kuchen
Blueberry Pinwheel Cobbler
Blackberry Bars
Oatmeal Raisin Ice Cream Sandwiches

Labor Day BBQ Menu

Marinated Grilled Shrimp
Grilled Stuffed Chili Cheddar Burgers
Chipotle Steak
Barbecue Corn
Basil Tomatoes
Scalloped Green Beans
Chili Bean Salad
English Pea Slaw
Minted Melon Balls
Deviled Eggs
Super Fast Garlic Bread Sticks
Strawberry Angel Food Trifle
Chocolate Cookie Ice Cream Sandwiches
Blackberry & Cream Parfaits

1 APPETIZERS

Appetizers play an integral role in setting the appetite of your guest. If serving fresh vegetables, allow about 1/2 cup vegetables per guest. For dip, allow about 1/4 cup serving per guest.

I serve appetizers at all functions. For informal gatherings, I have served just appetizers to my guest. They love the variety of food available. Serve 4-5 appetizers, a fruit and cheese plate and assorted cookies, brownies or petite cakes.

Brisket BBQ Poppers

Makes 24 poppers

12 jalapeno peppers
1 cup cream cheese, softened
1/2 cup grated Parmesan cheese
1 cup leftover brisket or steak, chopped
Black pepper and cayenne pepper to taste
24 thin slices cooked bacon

The bacon needs to be cooked but still pliable. Try using a one pound package of precooked bacon to cut the preparation time. Cut the jalapeno peppers in half. Remove all the seeds and veins. In a small bowl, add the cream cheese, Parmesan cheese and brisket. Stir until well combined. Season to taste with black pepper and cayenne pepper.

Spoon the mixture into each pepper half. Wrap a slice of bacon around each pepper. Secure the bacon with a toothpick. Preheat the oven to 450°. Place the poppers on a baking sheet. Bake for 10-15 minutes or until the poppers are hot and the cheese warm. Remove the poppers from the oven and serve. Remove the toothpicks before serving.

You can grill the poppers over medium coals for 5-6 minutes for a great smoky flavor.

Bacon Pepper Jack BBQ Chicken Wings

Serve these wings as an appetizer or for game day. They are so easy to make and super good!

Makes 24 wings

24 cooked barbecued wings (I use cooked frozen bbq wings)
12 slices Pepper Jack cheese
12 slices bacon

Preheat the oven to 450°. Cut each cheese slice in half. Wrap each cheese slice around a wing. Wrap the bacon around the cheese and secure with a toothpick if needed.

Bake for 12-15 minutes or until the bacon is crispy and the wings are hot. Remove the wings from the oven and serve.

Satan's Wings

Makes 18 appetizer servings

2 lbs. chicken wings
1/2 cup all purpose flour
1 1/8 tsp. salt
1/2 tsp. cayenne pepper
1/4 tsp. black pepper
Vegetable oil
1 tbs. red pepper flakes
2 tbs. lemon juice
2 tbs. Tabasco sauce
1/4 cup ketchup
2 tbs. vinegar
1/3 cup unsalted butter, melted

Split the chicken wings at the joints and discard the tips. In a plastic bag, add the all purpose flour, salt, cayenne pepper and black pepper. Shake the bag to combine the ingredients. Add 3 or 4 chicken wings at a time to the bag. Shake the bag to coat the wings with the mixture. Repeat until all the chicken wings are coated.

In a large skillet over medium heat, add oil to a 1" depth in the skillet. The oil needs to be 325°. When the oil is hot, add the chicken wings. Fry about 20 minutes or until the wings are done. Turn the wings to cook on both sides. Remove the wings from the skillet and drain them on paper towels.

To make the sauce for the wings, add the red pepper flakes, lemon juice, Tabasco sauce, ketchup and vinegar to a blender. Process until the pepper flakes are blended or about 30 seconds. Turn the blender to low and slowly add the melted butter. Blend the sauce on high speed until thick.

Remove the sauce from the blender and pour into a bowl. Add the wings and toss to coat the wings in the sauce.

Crispy Baked Buffalo Shrimp

The shrimp are a nice change from buffalo chicken wings.

Makes 24 shrimp

1/2 cup Tabasco sauce
1/4 cup melted unsalted butter
1 1/2 cups crushed butter crackers
24 large shrimp, peeled & deveined with tails left on
3/4 cup prepared ranch dressing
2 stalks celery

Preheat the oven to 350°. Spray a large baking sheet with non stick cooking spray. In a shallow bowl, add the cracker crumbs. In a separate small bowl, stir together the Tabasco sauce and butter.

Dip each shrimp in the Tabasco and butter. Roll each shrimp in the cracker crumbs. Place the shrimp on the prepared baking sheet. Bake for 15-20 minutes or until the shrimp are done and the coating crispy. Remove the shrimp from the oven and serve with the ranch dressing and celery sticks.

While the shrimp are cooking, cut each celery stalk into 12 thin sticks.

Marinated Meatballs

Makes about 40 meatballs

2 tbs. dry mustard
1/2 tsp. salt
1 tbs. Worcestershire sauce
1/4 tsp. black pepper
1/4 tsp. cayenne pepper
1/2 cup olive oil
1/2 cup tarragon vinegar
1 lb. ground beef
2 tbs. dried onion soup mix
1 egg
4 tbs. water
1 cup all purpose flour
2 tbs. vegetable oil

In a mixing bowl, add the dry mustard, salt, Worcestershire sauce, black pepper, cayenne pepper, olive oil and tarragon vinegar. Stir until combined. This will be the marinade for the meatballs.

In a separate bowl, add the ground beef, onion soup mix, egg and water. Using your hands, mix until well combined. Form the meatballs using about 1 teaspoon meat per meatball.

In a small bowl, add the all purpose flour. Roll the meatballs in the all purpose flour. In a skillet over medium heat, add the vegetable oil. Brown the meatballs in the vegetable oil. Cook the meatballs about 10 minutes or until the meatballs are well browned and done. Drain the grease from the skillet.

Pour the marinade over the meatballs. Place a lid on the skillet. Place the skillet in the refrigerator for 4 hours. When ready to serve, heat the meatballs in the skillet until thoroughly warmed. Pour the meatballs into a serving dish.

Marinated Shrimp

Makes 12 appetizer servings

2 lbs. shrimp, peeled and deveined
1 cup vegetable oil
1/4 cup olive oil
1 lemon, thinly sliced
1 tbs. lemon juice
1/4 cup red pimento, cut into thin strips
1/8 tsp. cayenne pepper
1/2 tsp. salt
3 dashes Worcestershire sauce
2 white onions, thinly sliced and rings separated
4 green onions, chopped including the green tops
Salt, black pepper and cayenne pepper to season

In a large pot, add about 3 quarts water over medium heat. The water will be used to cook the shrimp. Season the water with salt, black pepper and cayenne pepper to taste. Bring the water to a boil. When the water boils, add the shrimp. Cook the shrimp for 5 minutes or until the shrimp are done. Remove the pot from the heat and drain all the water from the shrimp. Run cold water over the shrimp.

Place the shrimp in a large serving bowl with a lid. In a large jar, add the vegetable oil, olive oil, lemon slices, lemon juice, red pimento, cayenne pepper, salt, Worcestershire sauce, onions and green onions. Stir until well combined. Pour the marinade over the shrimp. Cover the bowl and refrigerate for 24 hours. Stir the shrimp occasionally to keep the marinade combined.

Drain the marinade and place the shrimp on a serving platter. Arrange toothpicks around the shrimp to use for spears.

Shrimp with Herb Jalapeno Cheese

Makes 16 appetizers

32 large fresh shrimp, peeled, deveined but with tails left on
6 cups water
1/2 tsp. salt
8 oz. pkg. cream cheese, softened
1 garlic clove, minced
2 jalapeno peppers, seeded and minced
2 tsp. dried cilantro
Salt and black pepper to taste

In a large sauce pan, add the water and salt. Place the pan over medium heat. When the water boils, add the shrimp. Cook for 5 minutes or until the shrimp turn pink and are done. Remove the pan from the heat and drain all the water from the shrimp.

Run cold water over the shrimp and drain again. Pat the shrimp dry with paper towels. Place the shrimp in a bowl and refrigerate until well chilled.

In a mixing bowl, add the cream cheese, garlic, jalapeno peppers and cilantro. Stir until well combined. The mixture should be fluffy. Season to taste with salt and black pepper. Place the cream cheese mixture in a decorating bag. Pipe the cream cheese into the slits on the shrimp. The slits would be the part left open when the shrimp were deveined.

Sweet and Savory Sausage Balls

Makes 50 small appetizers

1 lb. ground pork sausage
1 cup apple butter
1/2 cup orange marmalade
3 tbs. lemon juice
1/4 tsp. salt
1/2 tsp. ground ginger

Preheat the oven to 400°. Form the sausage into 1" balls. Use about a teaspoon sausage for each ball. Place the sausage balls on a baking sheet.

Bake for 15 minutes or until the sausage balls are done and no longer pink. When the sausages are done, make the sauce. In a large saucepan over low heat, add the apple butter, orange marmalade, lemon juice, salt and ground ginger. Cook only until the orange marmalade is melted. Add the sausage balls and simmer for 15 minutes. Place the sausage balls and sauce in a chafing dish to serve.

Southern Sausage Balls

There is not a holiday occasion in the South that we do not serve sausage balls. They are a staple for holidays and brunch.

Makes about 60 sausage balls

1 lb. ground pork sausage
2 cups shredded sharp cheddar cheese
2 cups Bisquick
3 drops Tabasco sauce

Preheat the oven to 350°. Place a sheet of aluminum foil on two baking sheets. In a mixing bowl, add all the ingredients. Using your hands, mix until well combined.

The mixture will appear dry but keep mixing and it will come together. Form the mixture into 60 small balls about 1" in diameter. Place the sausage balls on the baking pans. Bake for 15-20 minutes. The sausage balls should be golden brown and the sausage done.

Remove the pans from the oven. Immediately remove the sausage balls from the pan. Serve hot or cold.

Corn Fritters with Cilantro Cream Sauce

Makes about 32 fritters

1 1/4 cups all purpose flour
1/2 cup yellow cornmeal
2 tsp. baking powder
1 tsp. chili powder
1/2 tsp. salt
1 cup frozen whole kernel corn, thawed
1 cup whole milk
1/3 cup chopped green bell pepper
1/4 cup chopped red onion
1 beaten egg
1 cup sour cream
1/4 cup chopped red bell pepper
1 tbs. minced fresh cilantro
1 tbs. lime juice
1/4 tsp. chili powder
Vegetable oil for frying

In a mixing bowl, add the all purpose flour, cornmeal, baking powder, chili powder and salt. Whisk until well combined. Stir in the corn, milk, green bell pepper, red onion and egg. Stir only until the batter is moistened.

Add the vegetable oil to a deep fryer or sauce pan. The vegetable oil needs to be about 3" deep in the pan. Heat the oil to 375°. Cook 4-5 fritters at a time. Do not over crowd the fritters in your pot. If you use a smaller pot, then only do 2-3 fritters at a time. Drop the fritter batter by tablespoonfuls into the hot oil. Cook for 3-4 minutes or until the fritters are done and golden brown. Remove the fritters from the oil and drain on paper towels.

Preheat the oven to 300°. Place the cooked fritters in a baking pan. Keep the fritters warm until ready to serve. I place the fritters in a crock pot set to warm or a chafing dish to serve. Serve with cilantro cream sauce.

You can make the sauce an hour ahead of time if desired. To make the dip, add the sour cream, red bell pepper, cilantro, lime juice and chili powder in a mixing bowl. Stir until well combined. Spoon the dip into a serving bowl. Refrigerate until ready to use.

Toasted Baguette Slices with Peach Salsa

Makes 24 appetizers

1 baguette, cut into 24 slices
8 oz. pkg. cream cheese, softened
3 tbs. minced fresh chives
3 large ripe peaches, peeled and finely chopped
3 tbs. vegetable oil
3 tbs. minced fresh mint
1/3 cup chopped fresh cilantro
1/4 cup minced red onion
2 tbs. minced jalapeno pepper
2 tbs. fresh lime juice
Salt and black pepper to taste

Preheat the oven to 350°. Place the baguette slices on a baking sheet. Toast the slices until warm and slightly browned.

In a small bowl, add the cream cheese and chives. Stir until well combined. Spread the cream cheese on the warm baguettes.

In a mixing bowl, add the peaches, vegetable oil, mint, cilantro, red onion, jalapeno pepper and lime juice. Stir until well combined. Season to taste with salt and black pepper. Spoon the salsa over the baguette slices to serve.

You can make the salsa up to 3 hours ahead if desired. The cream cheese can also be prepared ahead. Let the cream cheese soften before spreading. If made ahead, store the salsa and cream cheese in the refrigerator until ready to use.

Bacon Wands

Easy and so delicious! Make extra because they will disappear in a snap.

Makes 12 appetizers

12 slices bacon, thinly sliced
12 dry bread sticks

The bread sticks can be found in the bread aisle or near the spaghetti sauce. These are the dried bread sticks that come in plastic packages. You could make your own bread sticks and dry them out in the oven if desired.

Preheat the oven to 400°. Place a broiler rack over a baking pan. Do not place the bacon directly on the baking pan since the grease from the bacon will make the bread sticks soggy.

Wrap a slice of bacon around each bread stick. Place the bread sticks on the broiler rack in the baking pan. Bake for 10-15 minutes or until the bacon is crispy and done. Remove the bread sticks from the oven and serve hot.

Serve with a cheddar cheese or nacho dip if desired.

Baked Santa Fe Dip

I had this dip in Santa Fe, NM but it has become a staple for taco night and parties.

Makes 28 appetizer servings

2 cups shredded cheddar cheese
1 cup shredded Monterey Jack cheese
1 cup cooked whole kernel corn
1/2 cup mayonnaise
4 oz. can diced green chiles
2 tsp. finely chopped chipotle peppers in adobo sauce
1/4 tsp. garlic powder
1 tomato, seeded and chopped
1/4 cup sliced green onion
2 tbs. minced fresh cilantro, optional
Tortilla chips, raw sweet pepper slices, zucchini slices

Preheat the oven to 350°. Spray a 1 quart serving dish with non stick cooking spray. For parties, I use a decorative 9" pie plate. In a large bowl, add the cheddar cheese, Monterey Jack cheese, corn, mayonnaise, green chiles, chipotle peppers and garlic powder. Stir until well combined.

Spoon the dip into the serving plate. Bake for 25 minutes. The dip should be warm and the cheeses melted. Remove the dip from the oven. To garnish the dip, add the tomato, green onion and cilantro in a small bowl. Spoon the mixture in the center of the dip.

Serve the dip with tortilla chips, sweet pepper slices and zucchini slices.

You can make the dip up to 24 hours ahead. Do not bake the dip until ready to serve. Cover the unbaked dip and place in the refrigerator. Bake when ready to serve. Allow 5-10 extra minutes baking time for the dip if refrigerated.

Cumin Guacamole Dip

Makes 1 1/4 cups

2 tsp. cumin seeds
2 ripe avocados, peeled and diced
1 tsp. grated lime zest
1 tbs. lime juice
1/4 tsp. salt
1/8 tsp. ground red pepper
Vegetables or tortilla chips

In a skillet over medium heat, add the cumin seeds. Stir constantly and toast the cumin seeds for 2 minutes. You do not have to do this step but it vastly improves the taste of the dip. You can purchase toasted cumin seeds if desired.

Remove the skillet from the heat. Let the cumin seeds cool. Crush the cumin seeds. I use a meat cleaver and press down hard on the cumin seeds to crush them.

In a mixing bowl, add the avocados. Using a fork, mash the avocados until smooth. Add the lime zest, lime juice, salt, red pepper and cumin seeds. Stir until well combined. Spoon the dip into a serving bowl and serve with raw vegetables or tortilla chips.

We like to use this dip as a spread for hamburgers, steaks or quesadillas.

Shrimp Salsa

Makes about 8 cups

2 lbs. cooked shrimp, finely chopped
2 cups fresh cilantro, chopped
1/2 cup red onion, chopped
24 oz. jar mild salsa
2 cups fresh tomatoes, diced
2 tbs. fresh lime juice

Stir all the ingredients together in a large bowl. Cover the bowl and refrigerate at least 8 hours before serving. Serve with tortilla chips.

Pecan Cheese Log

Makes 12 servings

8 oz. pkg. cream cheese, softened
1 cup grated cheddar cheese
1 cup crumbled blue cheese
1/2 tsp. Tabasco sauce
1 cup chopped pecans

In a mixing bowl, add the cream cheese, cheddar cheese, blue cheese and Tabasco sauce. Using a heavy spoon, blend until well combined. Chill the cheese until it is firm enough to handle. Chilling time is about 2 hours.

When the cheeses are chilled, place the pecans on a large piece of plastic wrap. Shape the cheese mixture into an 8" log. Roll the log in the pecans. Wrap the cheese log in plastic wrap and chill until ready to serve. Serve with crackers.

Mama's Cheese Ball

This is the easiest cheese ball to make and my family devours them. Serve with an assortment of crackers or veggies.

8 oz. softened cream cheese
1 jar Kraft Old English Cheese Spread
1 tbs. dried minced onion
1 cup crushed pecans

In a mixing bowl, combine the cream cheese, Old English and the minced onions. Beat until fluffy with an electric mixer.

Place a sheet of plastic wrap on your kitchen counter. Place the crushed pecans on the plastic wrap. Scoop the cheese mixture from the mixing bowl and place on top of the pecans.

Using the sides of the plastic wrap like a glove, move the cheese mixture around the pecans until a ball forms and the cheese mixture is covered with pecans.

Place the cheese ball on a new piece of plastic wrap, wrap completely and chill the cheese ball overnight before serving.

Easy Onion Beef Triangles

My family loves these for game day munchies and I serve them as an appetizer at parties. They are so easy and the plate is always empty.

Makes 24 appetizers

6 slices pumpernickel bread
2 tbs. unsalted butter, softened
1 lb. shaved deli roast beef
1 cup canned fried onion rings
3 tbs. spicy mustard

Thinly spread the softened butter on one side of each bread slice. You can omit the butter if desired. It helps prevent the bread from getting soggy. Spread the mustard over the top of the butter. Place the shaved deli roast beef over the bread slices.

Cut each slice of bread in half diagonally. Cut each half into two triangles. Place the appetizers on a party tray. Place a few fried onion rings on top of each appetizer.

You can warm the appetizers in a 350° oven if desired. Sometimes I toast the bread with the butter before applying the rest of the toppings.

Sausage Mushrooms

Makes about 12-16 mushrooms

The amount may vary depending upon the size of the mushrooms in the package.

1 lb. pkg. fresh button mushrooms
1 lb. red hot pork sausage
1/2 cup grated cheddar cheese

Clean the mushrooms and remove the stem. Finely dice the stem. Preheat the oven to 375°. Make sure the cheese is grated and not shredded. If you are using shredded cheese, chop the cheese shreds into small pieces using a sharp knife.

In a mixing bowl, add the sausage, mushroom stems and cheddar cheese. Stir until well combined. Fill the mushroom caps with the sausage mixture. Bake for 30 minutes or until the sausage is done and the mushrooms are hot.

Note: You can prepare this dish up to 4 hours in advance. Bake the mushrooms before serving. These mushrooms are best fresh baked.

Crispy Cheddar Cubes

Makes 1 dozen appetizers

Make a double batch of these appetizers. I always make extra and my family devours them. Who does not love fried cheese? You can substitute whole milk mozzarella or any hard firm cheese if desired.

1 egg
3/4 cup fine dry seasoned bread crumbs
8 oz. cheddar cheese, cut into 1" cubes
Vegetable oil for frying
Paprika, optional

In a small bowl, add the egg and 1 tablespoon bread crumbs. Whisk until combined. Place the remaining bread crumbs in a shallow plate. Heat the vegetable oil in a deep fryer or sauce pan to 380°. The oil needs to be at least 2" deep.

Dip each cheese cube in the egg mixture. Let the excess egg drip off back into the bowl. Roll each cheese cube in the bread crumbs. Drop the cheese cubes, a few at a time, into the hot oil. Cook about 1 minute or until the bread crumbs are golden brown. Remove the cheese cubes from the oil and drain on paper towels.

Sprinkle the cheddar cubes with paprika if desired. Thread 2 cheese cubes on a toothpick. Repeat until all the cheese cubes are done. Serve hot. You do not have to place the cheese cubes on a toothpick but I find it makes them easier to serve.

Sugar Roasted Almonds

Makes 5 cups

4 cups whole almonds
1 egg white
1 tablespoon water
1/3 cup granulated sugar
1/3 cup light brown sugar
2 tsp. ground cinnamon
1/2 tsp. salt

Preheat the oven to 350°. Place the almonds on a baking sheet. Bake for 10 minutes. The almonds should be warm and lightly toasted. Remove the almonds from the oven and cool before using.

Turn the oven temperature to 325°. In a large bowl, add the egg white and water. Using a whisk, beat the egg white until well combined and frothy. Stir in the granulated sugar, brown sugar, cinnamon and salt.

Add the almonds and toss to combine the almonds with the egg white mixture. Line a jelly roll pan with parchment paper or aluminum foil. Spray the paper with non stick cooking spray. Spread the almonds, in a single layer, on the prepared pan. Bake for 20 minutes. The coating on the almonds should look dry. Remove the almonds from the oven and break up any clumps with a spoon.

Cool the almonds completely. Store the almonds in an airtight container. Store the almonds in the refrigerator. You can substitute mixed nuts, walnuts or pecans for the almonds if desired.

Southern Salted Pecans

Makes 4 cups

1 cup unsalted butter
4 cups pecan halves
1 tbs. salt

Preheat the oven to 200°. In a skillet over medium heat, add the butter. When the butter melts, add the pecans and salt. Stir to coat the pecans with the butter. Remove the skillet from the heat.

Spread the pecans on a 9 x 13 baking sheet. Bake for 1 hour. Stir every 15 minutes. Remove the pecans from the oven and cool completely before serving. Store the pecans in an airtight container.

Caramel Nut Corn

Makes 15 cups

12 cups popped popcorn
1 1/2 cups mixed salted nuts
1 cup light brown sugar
3/4 cup unsalted butter
1/2 cup dark corn syrup
1/2 tsp. baking soda

Spray a roasting pan with non stick cooking spray. Spray the pan well or the popcorn will stick. Place the popcorn and nuts in the roasting pan. They need to be warmed while you prepared the glaze.

Preheat the oven to 300° and keep the popcorn and nuts in the pan until the glaze is ready. In a large sauce pan over medium heat, add the brown sugar, butter and corn syrup. You must stir constantly while making the glaze. Bring the glaze to a boil. Cook for 12-17 minutes. On my stove, this takes about 16 minutes. The glaze will be thick and will form threads when dropped from a spoon.

Remove the pan from the heat and stir in the baking soda. The mixture will foam and rise tremendously. Pour the mixture over the popcorn and nuts. Stir until the popcorn and nuts are well coated. Bake for 15 minutes at 300°. Stir the popcorn to break up any pieces and bake for 5 more minutes.

Remove the popcorn from the oven and spread the popcorn on a large piece of aluminum foil. Cool the popcorn completely before serving. Break up any large pieces with your fingers. Store the popcorn in an airtight container up to 1 week.

2 MEATS

A variety of meats can be served at any holiday, barbecue or party. In my house, we usually serve, turkey, ham, prime rib or duck. Use whatever meats your family likes to serve for holidays.

Use a meat thermometer when cooking meat. Follow food safety precautions. Store leftover meat in the refrigerator and do not leave cooked food sitting out for long.

Roasting a turkey seems to be the one thing everyone fears at Thanksgiving. I have included the steps I use to roast a turkey. Anyone can roast a turkey. It just takes time and patience.

Hams are easy to bake. I buy fully cooked hams. Sometimes I buy the bone in and sometimes I buy boneless. Buy the ham your family likes best. Bake a ham with or without glaze. Even though the ham is fully cooked, I bake my hams. Bake fully cooked hams about 15 minutes per pound for a boneless ham and about 30 minutes per pound for a bone in ham.

How To Roast a Turkey

Wash everything the turkey touches with hot soap and water . Be sure to wash your hands frequently when handling any poultry. Always take extra food handling safety precautions when handling raw meat.

A stuffed turkey takes longer to cook than an unstuffed turkey. Allow about 20 minutes per pound for an unstuffed turkey and about 30 minutes per pound for a stuffed turkey. I do not stuff my turkey but serve my stuffing separately.

The turkey must be cooked to an internal temperature of 180°. Insert a meat thermometer in between the thigh and the breast to check the temperature. The juices should run clear when the turkey is done. Remove the turkey from the oven and let the turkey rest for 20 minutes before serving. Cover the turkey loosely with aluminum foil while the turkey is resting. You can buy a turkey with a built in thermometer but I always double check the turkey with a meat thermometer.

You can use an oven cooking bag to cook the turkey. I like to use the oven bags for turkey, chicken, duck and ham. The turkey stays juicier and clean up is a breeze. Follow the cooking bag instructions for your turkey. You can also place the turkey in the crock pot if you have a large enough crock pot.

I carve my turkey into slices and place on the table. I do not serve the whole turkey at the table. I remove the legs from the turkey and lay them on the serving plate for those who like turkey legs.

Thaw your turkey in the refrigerator. Allow 3-4 days in the refrigerator for a 15 lb. turkey. Rinse your thawed turkey with cold water. Remove any gizzards, livers or packets placed inside the cavity. Place 2 quartered onions and 3 stalks celery in the cavity of the turkey.

Season the turkey with salt and black pepper. You can use any seasonings you like on the turkey. Fresh rosemary sprigs placed inside the turkey and orange slices are very good. Lift the breast fat from the turkey and rub butter and seasonings liberally over the breast portion. I like to put rosemary sprigs or sage under the skin on the breast. Rub softened butter all over the turkey. Place the turkey in your roasting pan. Bake at 325° until the turkey is done.

Baste the turkey frequently with the pan juices or butter to promote even browning and maintain the juiciness of the turkey. You can easily over cook a turkey. Use a meat thermometer and watch the time closely.

Store leftover turkey in the refrigerator. Remove the turkey from the bone and place in an airtight container before placing in the refrigerator. I like to spoon some of the pan juices over the sliced turkey before placing the turkey in the refrigerator. This helps keep the turkey moist upon reheating. I throw away all leftovers after 72 hours.

Holiday Glazed Ham

Makes a 12 lb. ham

12 lb. fully cooked ham (boneless or bone in)
1 cup light brown sugar
1 tsp. dry mustard
1/4 tsp. ground cloves
2 tbs. cider vinegar

Bake the ham if desired before glazing. Even though the ham is fully cooked, I always bake my hams. If your ham will fit, place the ham in the crock pot to cook the ham.

To bake the ham, preheat the oven to 300°. Score the outside of the ham with a sharp knife. I make scores crosswise and then score across the lines making triangles. You can score the ham any way you choose. Place the ham in a roasting pan. Place 1 cup water in the bottom of the roasting pan. Cover the ham with aluminum foil. Bake for 3 hours.

Increase the heat to 350°. The glaze will only be placed on the ham during the last hour of cooking. To make the glaze, in a mixing bowl, stir together the brown sugar, mustard, cloves and vinegar. Brush or spoon 1/2 of the glaze over the ham. Bake for 1 hour. Glaze the ham every 15 minutes with the remaining glaze. Remove the ham from the oven and cool for 20 minutes before slicing.

Honey Orange Glazed Ham

Makes 12 servings

7 lb. cooked bone in ham
6 oz. can frozen orange juice concentrate, thawed
1 3/4 cups water
3/4 cup honey
1 1/2 tbs. cornstarch

Preheat the oven to 325°. Place the ham, fat side up in a 9 x 13 baking dish. In a sauce pan over medium heat, add the orange juice, water, honey and cornstarch. Stir constantly and bring the glaze to a slow boil. The glaze should be thickened. This will take about 5-7 minutes. Do not boil the glaze.

Pour half of the glaze over the ham. Bake the ham for 2 1/2 hours. Score the fat on the ham in a diamond pattern. Make the cuts about 1/4" deep on the ham. Spoon the remaining glaze over the ham. Bake for an additional 30-45 minutes or until the ham is fully cooked. Baste the ham several times during the last 30 minutes of cooking. Remove the ham from the oven and let the ham rest for 20 minutes before serving.

Pineapple Glazed Ham

Makes 12 servings

7 lb. fully cooked bone in ham
15 oz. can pineapple slices
1/4 cup light brown sugar
1/4 cup honey
Maraschino cherries
Whole cloves

Preheat the oven to 325°. Place the ham in a roasting pan. Cover the ham loosely with aluminum foil. Bake for 3 hours.

Drain the pineapple but reserve 1/4 cup juice. In a sauce pan over low heat, add the pineapple juice, brown sugar and honey. Heat only until the sugar dissolves. Remove the ham from the oven and score the ham all over with a sharp knife. Score the ham about 1/4" deep. Brush the glaze over the ham.

Arrange the pineapple slices over the ham. Hold the pineapple slices to the ham with toothpicks if needed. Place a maraschino cherry in the center of each pineapple slice. Secure the cherry with a toothpick if needed. Place the whole cloves over the ham. Brush more glaze over the ham. Bake for 30 minutes or until the glaze is hot and melted. Remove the ham from the oven. Remove all the toothpicks and cloves before serving. Allow the ham to rest for 20 minutes before serving.

Southern Stuffed Ham

The green pattern on the ham makes for a beautiful presentation.

Makes 12 servings

12 lb. fully cooked ham
10 oz. pkg. fresh spinach
8 green onions, finely chopped
1 cup minced fresh parsley
1 cup dry red wine
3/4 cup honey

Trim the thick skin if needed from the ham. With a sharp knife, make X cuts about 3" inches deep and 1" apart all over the ham.

Trim the stems and ends from the spinach. Finely chop the spinach. In a mixing bowl, add the spinach, green onions and parsley. Press the mixture into the cuts on the ham. Use your fingers and pack the greens well into the cuts.

Place the ham in a roasting pan. Preheat the oven to 325°. Brush the ham with the red wine. Bake for 2 1/2 hours. Brush several times with the wine while the ham bakes. Save 1/4 cup red wine and mix with the honey. Brush the wine honey glaze over the ham. Bake for 30 minutes. The ham should be hot when ready.

Remove the ham from the oven and brush again with any remaining wine honey glaze. Let the ham rest for 20 minutes before serving.

Apricot Glazed Ham

Makes 16 servings

8 lb. fully cooked ham
4 cups apricot nectar
2 cups applesauce
4 tbs. Worcestershire sauce
1 tsp. dry mustard
2 drops Tabasco sauce

Preheat the oven to 350°. Score the ham with a sharp knife. Place the ham in a roasting pan. In a mixing bowl, add the apricot nectar, applesauce, Worcestershire sauce, dry mustard and Tabasco sauce. Stir until well combined.

Pour the sauce over the ham. Cover the ham with aluminum foil and bake for 3 hours. Baste the ham frequently with the pan juices while cooking. Remove the ham from the oven and cool for 20 minutes before serving.

Spicy Prime Rib

Makes a 12 servings

6 lb. prime rib
12 garlic cloves, peeled
1/2 cup creole mustard
1/4 cup black pepper
Salt to season

The prime rib needs to marinate for 24 hours. Cut twelve slits in the sides and top of the prime rib. Insert a whole garlic clove in each slit. Season the prime rib with salt.

Brush the mustard all over the prime rib. Sprinkle the black pepper all over the prime rib. Place the prime rib in a roasting pan. Cover the prime rib with plastic wrap or aluminum foil. Marinate for 24 hours in the refrigerator.

Remove the prime rib from the refrigerator about 30 minutes before cooking. Let the prime rib sit at room temperature for 30 minutes. Preheat the oven to 450°. Place the prime rib in the oven and cook for 15 minutes. Reduce the heat to 350°. Baste the prime rib every 15 minutes with the pan juices. Be sure to baste the ends so they retain their moisture. Cook the prime rib to desired taste. The internal temperature needs to be at least 130° for rare. Test the temperature on the prime rib with a meat thermometer. Remove the prime rib from the oven when cooked to your specifications. Cool for 10 minutes before slicing.

I cut my prime rib into two equal portions. Some in my family like it medium and some like it well done. Cook about 20 minutes per pound or until the prime rib is done to your taste.

In my oven, medium rare prime rib takes about 1 1/2 hours.

Roast Duck

Makes 12 servings

3 frozen ducks, thawed, about 4 lbs. each duck
2 tsp. salt
1/4 tsp. black pepper
3 onions, peeled and quartered

Ducks produce a lot of fat while cooking. Prick the skin several times during baking to allow the fat to escape into the roasting pan. If the duck fat builds up too much in the roasting pan, it will smoke. Ladle the duck fat from the roasting pan into a bowl as the duck cooks. Save the duck fat for biscuits or other recipes.

Wash the ducks with cold water. Dry the ducks with a paper towel. Preheat the oven to 325°. Season the ducks with salt and black pepper. Place the onions in the cavity of the ducks.

Place the ducks in a roasting pan. With a fork, prick the skin of the ducks several times. Roast for 3 hours or until the drumsticks of the duck move easily. The ducks should be tender and golden brown when ready. Remove the ducks from the oven and cool for 5 minutes before serving.

Pineapple Roast Duck

Makes 8 servings

2 frozen ducks, thawed, about 5 lbs. each
20 oz. can sliced pineapple
1/4 cup melted unsalted butter
1/4 cup soy sauce
1/4 cup honey

Wash the ducks inside and out with cold water. Pat the ducks dry with paper towels.

Ducks produce a lot of fat while cooking. Prick the skin several times during baking to allow the fat to escape into the roasting pan. If the duck fat builds up too much in the roasting pan, it will smoke. Ladle the duck fat from the roasting pan into a bowl as the duck cooks. Save the duck fat for biscuits or other recipes.

Place the ducks in a roasting pan. Preheat the oven to 325°. Drain the pineapple slices but reserve the juice. Place the pineapple slices over the ducks. Secure the pineapple slices with toothpicks if needed.

Roast the ducks for 1 1/2 hours. Remove all drippings from the pan. In a small bowl, add the melted butter, soy sauce and honey. Stir until well combined. Brush the glaze over the ducks. Bake for 1 to 1 1/2 hours or until the drumsticks move easily and the duck is tender. The duck should be dark brown.

Brush the glaze over the duck a couple of times while baking during the last hour. Brush the reserved pineapple juice over the ducks. Remove the ducks from the oven and cool for 10 minutes before serving.

Fruited Roast Duck

Makes 12 servings

3 frozen ducks, thawed, about 4 lbs. each
1 tsp. salt
3 onions, peeled and quartered
1 apple, cored and cubed
16 oz. can whole figs
16 oz. can dark sweet cherries
6 oz. can frozen orange juice concentrate, thawed

Ducks produce a lot of fat while cooking. Prick the skin several times during baking to allow the fat to escape into the roasting pan. If the duck fat builds up too much in the roasting pan, it will smoke. Ladle the duck fat from the roasting pan into a bowl as the ducks cooks. Save the duck fat for biscuits or other recipes.

Wash the ducks with cold water. Dry the ducks with a paper towel. Preheat the oven to 325°. Season the ducks with salt. Place the onions and apple cubes in the cavity of the ducks.

Place the ducks in a roasting pan. With a fork, prick the skin of the ducks several times. Roast the ducks for 2 1/2 hours. Brush the ducks with the orange juice concentrate. Cook for 30-45 minutes or until the drumsticks of the ducks move easily. The ducks should be a rich golden brown. Remove the ducks from the oven and spoon the fruit sauce over the ducks before serving.

To make the fruit sauce, drain the figs and discard the liquid. Place the figs and the cherries with any juice in a sauce pan over low heat. Heat only until the fruit is warm. Remove the pan from the heat and serve over the ducks.

You can pour the sauce over the ducks while they are whole but I like to serve the sauce over cut pieces of duck.

Roast Goose with Fruit Stuffing

Makes 6 servings

9 lb. frozen goose, thawed
11 oz. pkg. mixed dried fruits, diced
1 cup orange juice
10 slices toasted white bread, diced
1/2 tsp. ground ginger
1/2 tsp. ground cinnamon
1/2 tsp. ground nutmeg
1/4 tsp. ground cloves

Remove the giblets and any large pieces of fat from the inside of the goose. Rinse the goose with cold water. Pat the goose dry with paper towels.

In a mixing bowl, add the dried mixed fruit and orange juice. Stir until combined and set aside for 30 minutes. Add the bread, ginger, cinnamon, nutmeg and cloves. Toss until combined. The stuffing will be dry at this point.

Stuff about 1 cup dressing in the neck cavity of the goose. Stuff the remaining dressing into the cavity of the goose. Close the goose with skewers. Place the goose on a broiler rack in a baking pan. Prick the goose in the fatty part around the legs and wings with a fork.

Preheat the oven to 325°. Roast the goose for 1 hour. Remove any pan drippings. Goose produce a lot of fat so you will have to remove the pan drippings several times. If you do not remove pan drippings, they will smoke and cause a mess.

Roast the goose about 3 hours. The goose should be done and tender. During the last 30 minutes of cooking time, brush pan drippings over the goose. The goose should be golden brown. Remove the goose from the oven and let it rest for 15 minutes before slicing.

Roast Goose with Stewed Apples

Makes 12 servings

12 lb. frozen goose, thawed
Salt to season
4 1/2 cups water
1/2 onion, sliced
6 peppercorns
1/2 cup plus 2 tbs. unsalted butter
2 lbs. apples, peeled and cored
1/2 cup granulated sugar
1/2 cup white wine
1 tbs. fresh lemon juice
Large strip lemon peel

Wash the goose inside and out with cold water. Pat the goose dry with paper towels. Place the goose on a broiler rack in a roasting pan. Season the goose inside and out with salt. Close the cavity of the goose with skewers. Pour 4 cups water, onion and peppercorns into the roasting pan. Roast the goose about 4 hours.

The legs of the goose should move easily when done and the goose should be golden brown. Baste the goose with 1/2 cup butter during the last hour of cooking. Remove the goose from the oven to rest while you make the apples.

In a large skillet over medium heat, add 2 tablespoons butter and the apples. Saute the apples for 3 minutes. Add 1/2 cup water, granulated sugar, wine, lemon juice and lemon peel. Bring the apples to a boil. Place a lid on the skillet and reduce the heat to low. Simmer the apples about 10 minutes or until they are tender. Remove the lemon peel and serve the apples with the goose.

You can make a gravy for the goose if desired. Use the Pan Drippings Gravy recipe in this book.

Italian Baked Shrimp

Serve these shrimp as a main course or appetizer for New Year's Eve or a New Year's Brunch.

Makes 8 main dish servings or 20 appetizer servings

1/4 cup unsalted butter
8 oz. bottle Italian salad dressing
4 tbs. fresh lemon juice
1/4 tsp. black pepper
3 lbs. large shrimp with tails, peeled and deveined

Preheat the oven to 325°. In a 9 x 13 baking pan, add the butter. Place the pan in the oven until the butter melts. Add the Italian dressing, lemon juice and black pepper to the butter. Stir until combined.

Add the shrimp to the sauce. Toss the shrimp to coat with the sauce. Bake for 15-25 minutes. Stir the shrimp several times to coat the shrimp while baking. Cook only until the shrimp are done and have turned pink. Do not over cook the shrimp. Spoon the shrimp on a serving platter.

Marinated Grilled Shrimp

Serve these flavorful shrimp at any party or barbecue.

Makes 6 servings

1/3 cup cooking sherry
1/3 cup sesame seed oil
1/3 cup soy sauce
1/2 tsp. granulated sugar
1/4 tsp. garlic powder
1/4 tsp. ground ginger
2 lbs. large fresh shrimp, peeled and deveined

In a shallow bowl, add the cooking sherry, sesame seed oil, soy sauce, granulated sugar, garlic powder and ginger. Stir until well combined. Add the shrimp and toss to coat the shrimp in the marinade. Cover the bowl with a lid or plastic wrap. Marinate the shrimp in the refrigerator for 3 hours.

Drain the shrimp but reserve the marinade. Place the shrimp on skewers. Grill over medium coals about 6-8 minutes or until the shrimp are done. Do not over cook the shrimp. Baste the shrimp frequently with the marinade during cooking.

Southern Barbecue Shrimp

Makes 6 servings

Wooden skewers
2 lbs. jumbo shrimp, peeled and deveined
1 cup melted unsalted butter
1/2 cup Worcestershire sauce
1/2 cup fresh lemon juice
1 tbs. grated lemon zest
3 tbs. light brown sugar
5 tbs. Old Bay seasoning

Soak the wooden skewers for one hour in water. If you are using metal skewers, you do not have to soak them.

In a large mixing bowl, add the butter, Worcestershire sauce, lemon juice, lemon zest, brown sugar and Old Bay seasoning. Stir until well combined.

Place the shrimp on skewers. Place the skewers in a large shallow baking dish. Pour the marinade over the shrimp. Cover the dish with plastic wrap and refrigerate the shrimp for 2 hours.

Remove the shrimp from the refrigerator. Place the shrimp over hot coals. Grill for 2-3 minutes on each side or until the shrimp are done. Discard the marinade.

Herb Marinated Salmon

Makes 8 servings

8 salmon fillets
3 tbs. lime juice
2 tbs. olive oil
2 tbs. minced fresh parsley
1 tsp. dried thyme
1 tsp. black pepper

Place the salmon fillets in a plastic bag. In a small bowl, add the lime juice, olive oil, parsley, thyme and black pepper. Stir until combined. Pour the marinade over the fillets. Close the bag and shake the bag to cover the salmon with the marinade.

Marinate the salmon in the refrigerator for 20 minutes. Bake, fry or grill the salmon about 4 minutes on each side as desired. They are delicious on the grill. Cook the salmon only until the salmon flakes easily with a fork.

Texas Game Hens

I fix these Cornish hens for brunch. They are easy to make and they allow me to enjoy my guest.

4 Cornish hens, about 1 lb. each
1/2 tsp. salt
1/2 tsp. garlic powder
1 tsp. chili powder
1/2 cup apple jelly
1/2 cup ketchup
1 tbs. vinegar

Rinse the hens and pat them dry with a paper towel. Preheat the oven to 350°. Split the hens in half. Sprinkle the salt, garlic powder and 1/2 teaspoon chili powder over the hens. Place the hens in a roasting pan with the skin side up.

Bake for 1 hour or until the juices run clear and the hens are done. The internal temperature needs to be 180°. Baste the hens every 15 minutes with the pan juices.

The hens need to be glazed during the last 15 minutes cooking time. In a small microwavable bowl, add the apple jelly, 1/2 teaspoon chili powder, ketchup and vinegar. Heat only until the jelly melts. Stir until the glaze is combined. Brush the glaze over the hens during the last 15 minutes of cooking time. Baste every 5 minutes for 15 minutes. Remove the hens from the oven and let the hens rest for 5 minutes before serving.

You can roast the hens in the crock pot if desired. Place the hens on a rack or balls of aluminum foil. Season as directed above. Set the crock pot to high and cook for 3-4 hours. Glaze several times during the last hour of cooking.

Grilled Cumin Chicken

Makes 8 servings

2 whole chickens, about 3 lbs. each
6 tbs. lemon juice
2 tbs. vegetable oil
2 tbs. ground cumin
1 tbs. salt
1 tbs. black pepper
2 tsp. celery salt
1/4 tsp. cayenne pepper

Quarter each chicken. Rinse the chicken with cold water and pat the chicken quarters dry with paper towels. Place the chicken quarters in a large shallow baking dish. Pour the lemon juice over the chicken. Cover the dish with plastic wrap or a lid. Marinate the chicken in the refrigerator for 3 hours.

Remove the chicken from the lemon juice. Rub the vegetable oil over the chicken. Combine the ground cumin, salt, black pepper, celery salt and cayenne pepper in a small bowl. Sprinkle the seasonings over both sides of the chicken.

Place the chicken quarters over medium hot coals. Grill for 30-40 minutes or until the chicken quarters are done and tender. Turn the chicken a couple of times during the grilling process for even cooking.

Grilled Georgia Peach BBQ Chicken

Makes 4 servings

4 boneless skinless chicken breast
2 tsp. onion salt
1/3 cup peach preserves
3 tbs. barbecue sauce
4 peaches, sliced
2 tbs. unsalted butter, melted

Sprinkle the chicken with 1 teaspoon onion salt. In a small bowl, add 1 teaspoon onion salt, peach preserves and barbecue sauce. Stir until combined. Place the chicken over medium coals. Grill the chicken for 10-15 minutes or until the chicken is done and tender. Glaze the chicken during cooking with the peach preserve sauce. Remove the chicken from the grill and let the chicken rest while you prepare the peaches.

Brush the peach slices with butter. Place the peaches, cut side down, on the grill. Grill for 4-5 minutes. The peaches should have grill marks and be tender. Serve with the chicken.

Grilled Beef Tenderloin with Mushrooms

Serve for a New Year's party or any barbeque. Your guest will be impressed.

Makes 8-10 servings

4 cups sliced fresh mushrooms
1 cup chopped green onions
1/4 cup unsalted butter, melted
1/4 cup minced fresh parsley
6 lb. beef tenderloin
1/2 tsp. season salt
1/4 tsp. lemon pepper seasoning
1 cup crumbled blue cheese
8 oz. bottle red wine vinegar and oil dressing
Crushed peppercorns

In a skillet over medium heat, add the mushrooms, green onions and butter. Saute the vegetables for 5 minutes. The mushrooms should be tender. Stir in the parsley and remove the pan from the heat.

Trim the excess fat from the tenderloin. Cut the tenderloin lengthwise to about 1/4" of the edges. You need to make a pocket for the mushrooms. Spread the tenderloin open if necessary. Sprinkle the season salt and lemon pepper over the tenderloin.

Spoon the mushroom mixture into the center of the tenderloin. Sprinkle the blue cheese over the mushrooms. Tie the tenderloin together with butcher string or close with toothpicks. Place the tenderloin in a large baking dish with a lid. Pour the red wine vinegar and oil dressing over the tenderloin. Cover the dish with a lid or plastic wrap. Marinate the tenderloin for 8 hours. Spoon the marinade occasionally over the tenderloin.

Remove the tenderloin from the marinade. Press the peppercorns into the tenderloin. Have your grill hot and ready. Place the tenderloin over hot coals. Cook for 35-45 minutes or until a meat thermometer registers 160°. The tenderloin should be medium done. You can cook the tenderloin to your taste. If you like the tenderloin rare, cook for less time. If you like your tenderloin well done, cook for more time.

Remove the tenderloin from the grill and remove the tie strings or toothpicks. Let the tenderloin rest for 10 minutes before serving.

Coca Cola Beef Brisket

You can cook the brisket in the oven, crock pot or smoker.

Makes 6 servings

1 liter bottle Coca Cola
1 1/2 cups water
3 lb. beef brisket
1 cup tomato sauce
1 pkg. dry onion soup mix
1/8 tsp. ground ginger
Salt and black pepper to season

Preheat the oven to 350°. Trim the fat from the brisket if desired. Season the meat with salt and black pepper if desired. Place the brisket in a roasting pan. Rub the onion soup mix on the brisket. Pour the tomato sauce over the brisket. Pour the Coca Cola over the brisket. Sprinkle the ginger over the top of the brisket. Pour the water around the brisket in the pan.

Cover the pan with a lid or aluminum foil. Bake for 3-4 hours or until the brisket is tender. Baste the brisket with the pan juices several times during the cooking process. Remove the brisket from the oven. Let the brisket rest covered for 10 minutes.

Remove the aluminum foil or lid. Remove the brisket and cut the brisket into slices to serve. Serve some of the pan drippings over the brisket if desired.

Crock Pot: Follow directions above but omit the water. Cook on low for 7-8 hours.

Grill: Follow the directions above but place the roasting pan in the smoker. Cook for 4-6 hours or until the brisket is tender.

Chipotle Steak

Makes 4 servings

3/4 cup steak sauce
4 boneless beef ribeye steaks, about 8 oz. each
2 tbs. fresh lime juice
3 tbs. chipotle peppers in adobo sauce, chopped
1/3 cup unsalted butter, softened

In a small bowl, add the steak sauce, lime juice and 1 tablespoon chipotle peppers. Stir until well combined. Pour half of the mixture into a separate small bowl to use for a glaze.

Place the steaks in a plastic bag. Pour half of the steak sauce mixture over the steaks. Seal the bag and squeeze the bag to cover the steaks with the marinade. Marinate for 1 hour in the refrigerator.

In a small bowl, add 2 tablespoons chipotle peppers and the butter. Stir until well combined. Refrigerate for use later in the recipe. Remove the steaks from the refrigerator and let them sit at room temperature for 20 minutes.

Place the steaks over medium hot coals and grill until done to your taste. Brush the steaks with half of the steak sauce during cooking. Remove the steaks from the grill and place the butter chipotle mixture over each hot steak.

Flank Steak Pinwheels

Makes 8 servings

2 flank steaks, about 1 1/4 lbs. each
2 cups chopped onion
1 cup vegetable oil
2/3 cup vinegar
4 garlic cloves, minced
2 tsp. salt
1/2 tsp. dried thyme
1/2 tsp. dried marjoram
1/8 tsp. black pepper

Cut the flank steaks diagonally across the grain into 1/4" thick slices. Roll each slice up like a jelly roll. Close the ends with toothpicks. Place the slices in a 9 x 13 baking dish.

In a small bowl, add the vegetable oil, vinegar, garlic, salt, thyme, marjoram and black pepper. Whisk until combined. Sprinkle the onion over the steaks. Pour the marinade over the steaks. Cover the pan with a lid or plastic wrap. Marinate for 8 hours.

Remove the slices from the marinade. Grill over hot coals for 10-12 minutes or until the steaks are done to your taste. Turn the slices often for even cooking.

Chili Orange Glazed Baby Back Ribs

Makes 4 servings

4 lbs. baby back ribs
2 cups orange juice
1/2 cup chili sauce
2 tbs. hoisin sauce
1 tbs. grated orange zest
1 tbs. Tabasco sauce
2 tsp. light brown sugar

Place ribs in a large baking dish. Pour the orange juice over the ribs. Cover the dish with plastic wrap. Marinate for 2 hours in the refrigerator. Remove the ribs from the refrigerator and let them sit at room temperature for 20 minutes.

Remove the ribs from the pan and pat them dry. Place the ribs over indirect heat over medium coals. Cook about 1 1/2 to 2 hours. The ribs should be done and tender.

To make the glaze, add the chili sauce, hoisin sauce, orange zest, Tabasco sauce and brown sugar to a mixing bowl. Stir until well combined. Brush the glaze on the ribs several times during the last 30 minutes of cooking.

The glaze has a high sugar content and will burn easily so watch the glaze carefully.

Grilled Stuffed Chili Cheddar Burgers

Makes 8 servings

2 1/2 lbs. ground beef
2 tbs. Worcestershire sauce
2 tsp. salt
1/2 tsp. black pepper
1/2 tsp. garlic powder
2 cups shredded cheddar cheese
1/2 cup chili sauce
1/8 tsp. chili powder
8 hamburger buns, buttered and toasted

In a mixing bowl, add the ground beef, Worcestershire sauce, salt, black pepper and garlic powder. Use your hands and mix until well combined. Form the meat mixture into 16 patties about 4" in size.

In a small bowl, add the cheddar cheese, chili sauce and chili powder. Stir until well combined. Place about 1/4 cup of the cheese mixture in the center of 8 patties. Place the remaining patties on top of the cheese mixture and seal the edges. Pinch the edges together with your fingers. Make certain the edges are sealed or the center will leak out.

Grill the burgers over slow coals cook about 7-9 minutes per side or until the burgers are done and no longer pink.

Place the burgers on buns and serve.

Grilled Mushroom Burgers

Makes 6 servings

1/2 cup buttermilk
1/3 cup seasoned bread crumbs
3 oz. can sliced mushrooms, drained
2 tsp. dried minced onion
1 tsp. season salt
1 lb. ground beef

In a mixing bowl, add all the ingredients. Use your hands and mix until well combined. Form the burgers into 6 patties. Place the burgers on a grill over medium coals.

Grill the burgers about 5-6 minutes on each side or until the beef is done and no longer pink. Serve on buns if desired with your favorite burger fixings.

Country Pork and Black Eye Peas

We eat this on New Year's Day and several times during the year. Serve with cornbread, iced tea and greens for a hearty meal.

Makes 6 servings

1 lb. dried black eye peas
4 lb. cooked smoked pork picnic shoulder
Salt and black pepper to taste

Place the black eye peas in a large pot. Pick out any bad peas. Cover the peas with water to 3" above the peas. Let the peas soak for 24 hours. When the peas have soaked, drain off the soaking water. Rinse the peas with cold water.

In a dutch oven, add the pork shoulder. Cover the pork shoulder with water. Place the pan over medium heat. Bring the shoulder to a boil. Place a lid on the pan and simmer for 1 1/2 hours. Add the peas to the pan. Bring the mixture back to a boil. Reduce the heat to medium low. Place the lid back on the pan and simmer for 1 1/2 hours. The pork should be fork tender and the peas done.

As each stove cooks differently, cook until the pork is tender and the peas done. The time listed is for my stove. Remove the pork from the pot. Cut away the skin and discard. Shred the meat and add the pork back to the pot. Serve with hot cornbread and greens. Smoked pork shoulders are salty. Season the peas and pork with salt and black pepper if desired.

Dixie Pork and Sweets

This is another wonderful dish to serve on New Year's. Serve as a meal or for brunch.

Makes 8 servings

8 sweet potatoes, peeled and quartered
3 lbs. pork shoulder, cubed
2 tbs. vegetable shortening
3 onions, sliced
4 red apples, cored and sliced into rings
2 tbs. light brown sugar
3 tbs. all purpose flour
2 tsp. salt
1 tsp. dried marjoram
1/4 tsp. black pepper
3 cups apple juice
3 tbs. vegetable oil, optional

Place the sweet potatoes in a large sauce pan. Cover the sweet potatoes with water. Place the pan over medium heat and cook for 15-20 minutes. The sweet potatoes should be tender. Remove the sweet potatoes from the heat and drain all the water from the pan.

Trim all the fat from the pork. In a large skillet over medium heat, add the pork cubes and 2 tablespoon vegetable shortening. Brown the pork cubes for 10 minutes. Make sure all sides of the pork are well browned.

In a 9 x 13 baking dish, add the sweet potatoes. Spoon half of the pork cubes over the sweet potatoes. Place half of the onion slices and apples over the pork. Sprinkle 1 tablespoon brown sugar over the apple rings.

Repeat with another layer of pork, onion slices, apple rings and brown sugar. Measure your pan drippings from browning the pork. You need 3 tablespoons pan drippings. Add the vegetable oil if needed. Place the skillet back over medium heat. Stir in the all purpose flour, salt, marjoram, black pepper and apple juice. Stir constantly and cook until the sauce thickens and bubbles. Cook for 1 minute after the sauce bubbles. Remove the pan from the heat and pour over the ingredients in the baking dish. Cover the dish with a lid or aluminum foil. Refrigerate the dish for 1 hour. Remove the dish from the refrigerator and let it sit at room temperature for 30 minutes.

Preheat the oven to 350°. Bake for 2 hours or until the pork is done and tender. Remove the pan from the oven and cool for 5 minutes before serving.

To serve for brunch, remove the pork to a serving platter. Spoon the sweet potatoes and apple slices around the pork.

Hoppin' John

A New Year's day must have but delicious any time of the year.

Makes 6-8 servings

2 cups dried black eye peas
12 cups water
1 smoked ham hock
1 1/2 cups chopped onion
2 cups long grain white rice, uncooked
Salt and black pepper to taste

Wash the dried peas in water until clean. Place the peas in a large pot with the water, ham hock and the onion. Simmer the peas uncovered on medium low heat about 1 1/2 hours. Be sure to keep the peas covered with water while cooking. After cooking, you should have about 3-4 cups of water left in the peas. If you do not have enough water, add water to the pot and bring the peas back to a low simmer.

Add the uncooked rice and cover the pot with a lid. Simmer on low about 20 minutes or until the rice is cooked. Remove the pan from the heat and let the pan sit for 15 minutes. Fluff the peas and rice with a fork and serve with hot buttered cornbread muffins.

This is an easy crock pot dish. Double the cooking times based on your crock pot and cook on high or low temperature.

3 STUFFING & DRESSINGS

Dressings and stuffing are a must at Thanksgiving. The stuffing can be sweet or savory. Stuffing should be moist but not gummy. Included you will find recipes for Southern dressing and stuffing favorites.

Don't just save the stuffing recipes for the holidays. They are easy to make especially when you have extra stale bread on hand. They make a great side dish to any dinner meal.

Every oven cooks differently and you may need to add additional liquid to your stuffing to keep it moist. I do not use stuffing in a turkey or poultry. Stuff your turkey or poultry if desired.

I list instructions to bake the stuffing separately if desired.

Southern Cornbread Dressing

Makes 12 servings

This recipe saves a lot of chopping. I make this dressing every Thanksgiving, Christmas and Easter. It taste and looks just like old fashioned dressing. My family loves it.

4 tbs. bacon grease
4 cups yellow or white self rising cornmeal
6 eggs
1-2 cups whole milk
10.75 oz. can cream of mushroom soup
10.75 oz. can cream of chicken soup
10.75 oz. can cream of celery soup
6-8 cups chicken broth
1 pkg. onion soup mix
2-3 tsp. dry rubbed sage

Preheat the oven to 450°. Grease a 9 x 13 baking pan or two 9" iron skillets with bacon grease. Place the pan in the oven to melt the grease and heat the pan. To make cornbread, you always need a hot pan before adding the batter.

In a large mixing bowl, add the self rising cornmeal and 6 eggs. Add only enough of the milk to make a cornbread batter. You want the batter to be thick but not so thick that you can not pour the batter into the pan. The batter should resemble the consistency of cake batter. Let the batter rest for 3 minutes. The cornmeal will absorb the milk as it rest. Add additional milk if need to make a batter.

Remove the baking pan or iron skillets from the oven. Pour the cornbread batter into the pans. Bake about 20-25 minutes or until the cornbread is done and golden brown. When the cornbread is done, remove the pan from the oven and let the cornbread cool in the pan.

In a large roasting pan or baking dish, crumble the cornbread. Add the chicken soup, mushroom soup, celery soup, onion soup mix and 2 teaspoons sage to the cornbread in the pan. Heat the chicken broth in a saucepan on the stove. Pour the chicken broth slowly over the cornbread and begin to stir. Use 5-6 cups chicken broth in the beginning. Mix well making certain all the ingredients are combined. Add additional chicken broth as needed to make a moist dressing. You do not want the dressing to be runny from extra chicken broth, but you do want it moist. While the dressing is baking in the oven, the cornbread will absorb some additional moisture.

Taste the cornbread dressing and season with additional sage, salt and pepper if desired. The sage taste will be a little stronger after it is cooked. My family likes a strong sage taste, so I use 3 teaspoons.

Preheat your oven to 350°. Place the roasting pan with the dressing in the oven and bake for 30-45 minutes. The dressing will be hot in the center and begin to brown on top when done. Do not overcook the dressing or it will be dry.

Baked Fruit Dressing

This is delicious with turkey, chicken, duck or quail. Serve for dessert with ice cream or whipped cream.

Makes 10 servings

15 oz. can sliced peaches, drained
16 oz. can sliced pears, drained
15 oz. can pineapple tidbits, drained
1/3 cup raisins
1/3 cup chopped walnuts
3/4 cup light brown sugar
1 tsp. vanilla extract
15 oz. can apricot halves, drained
5 cups bread, cubed and toasted
3/4 cup melted unsalted butter

Preheat the oven to 325°. Spray a 9 x 13 baking pan with non stick cooking spray. Add the peaches, pears, pineapple, raisins, walnuts, 1/2 cup light brown sugar and vanilla extract to the baking pan. Stir until well combined. Arrange the apricot halves, pit side down, over the top of the fruit.

Sprinkle the bread slices over the fruit. In a small bowl, stir together 1/4 cup light brown sugar and the butter. Pour the butter over the bread cubes. Bake for 25-35 minutes or until the dressing is hot and the bread golden brown. Serve warm.

Sausage Cornbread Stuffing

Makes 12 servings

3/4 lb. ground pork sausage
3/4 cup finely chopped onion
1/2 cup chopped green bell pepper
1/2 cup chopped celery
1/2 cup unsalted butter
5 cups dry bread cubes
4 1/2 cups crumbled cooked cornbread
3/4 cup toasted chopped pecans
1 tsp. poultry seasoning
1/8 tsp. black pepper
1 to 1 1/2 cups chicken broth

In a large skillet over medium heat, add the pork sausage. Stir frequently to break the sausage into crumbles as it cooks. Cook the sausage for 6-7 minutes or until the sausage is done and no longer pink. Remove the sausage from the the skillet and drain off the excess grease.

In the skillet used to cook the sausage, add the onion, green bell pepper, celery and butter. Stir frequently and cook the vegetables for 4 minutes. Remove the skillet from the heat.

In a large mixing bowl, add the bread cubes, cornbread, sausage, onion mixture, pecans, poultry seasoning, black pepper and 1 cup chicken broth. Toss until the ingredients are combined and moistened. Add the remaining chicken broth if needed to make a moist stuffing.

This recipe will stuff a 12 lb. turkey. To cook the stuffing separately, spray a 2 quart casserole dish with non stick cooking spray. Spoon the stuffing into the prepared casserole dish. Cover the dish with a lid or aluminum foil. Preheat the oven to 325°. Bake for 35-45 minutes. The stuffing should be set and hot.

Sausage Bread Stuffing

Makes about 6 cups stuffing

8 oz. ground pork sausage
4 cups bread, cubed
2 tbs. whole milk
1 cup diced celery
1/2 tsp. salt
1/2 tsp. poultry seasoning
1/8 tsp. black pepper

In a skillet over medium heat, add the pork sausage. Stir the sausage frequently to break the sausage into crumbles as it cooks. Cook for 6-7 minutes or until the sausage is done and no longer pink.

Remove the sausage from the skillet but leave the pan drippings in the skillet. Place the sausage and bread in a mixing bowl. Drizzle the milk over the bread. Add the celery to the pan drippings. Saute the celery for 5 minutes. Stir in the salt, poultry seasoning and black pepper. Remove the skillet from the heat and pour the mixture over the bread cubes. Toss until the bread cubes are moistened.

Preheat the oven to 350°. Spoon the stuffing into a 2 quart casserole dish. Bake for 20 minutes or until the stuffing is set and lightly browned.

Raisin Walnut Stuffing

Makes about 10 cups stuffing or enough to stuff a 12 lb. turkey

2 cups seedless raisins
1 1/2 cups water
2 cups chopped celery
1 large onion, chopped
1/2 cup unsalted butter
1 tsp. granulated chicken bouillon
1 tsp. salt
1 tsp. rubbed sage
1/4 tsp. black pepper
8 cups bread, cubed
2 cups chopped walnuts

Place the raisins and water in a sauce pan. Place the sauce pan over medium heat and bring to a boil. Boil for 1 minute. Remove the pan from the heat.

In a skillet over medium heat, add the celery, onion and butter. Saute the onion and celery about 5 minutes. Stir in the chicken bouillon, salt, sage and black pepper. Remove the pan from the heat.

In a large mixing bowl, add the bread cubes. Pour the raisins and water over the bread. Add the celery and onion mixture along with the walnuts. Toss until combined and the bread is moistened.

Preheat the oven to 350°. Spoon the stuffing into a 3 quart casserole dish. Bake for 20-30 minutes. The stuffing should be hot and set.

Old Fashioned Potato Stuffing

Makes about 12 cups or enough to stuff a 14 lb. turkey

1/2 cup vegetable shortening
1/2 cup unsalted butter
16 cups peeled and diced potatoes
3 large onions, chopped
1 cup thinly sliced celery
4 tsp. salt
1/2 tsp. black pepper
1/2 cup whole milk
3 cups dry bread crumbs
4 eggs
6 tbs. minced fresh parsley

In a large skillet or dutch oven over medium heat, add the vegetable shortening and butter. When the shortening and butter melts, stir in the potatoes, onions, celery, salt and black pepper. Stir frequently and cook until the potatoes begin to brown. Reduce the heat to low. Place a lid on the skillet and cook about 20 minutes. Stir occasionally to keep the potatoes, onion and celery from sticking to the skillet. The potatoes should be tender when ready.

Stir in the milk, bread crumbs, eggs and parsley. Stir constantly and cook until the eggs are cooked. You will see small pieces of the egg in the stuffing. Remove the pan from the heat.

To bake the stuffing, preheat the oven to 350°. Spoon the stuffing into a 3 quart rectangular baking dish. Bake for 25-30 minutes. The stuffing should be hot and set when ready.

Oyster Stuffing

Makes about 8 cups stuffing or enough for a 10 lb. turkey

1 bay leaf
1/2 cup chopped celery
1/2 cup chopped onion
1/4 cup unsalted butter
6 cups dry bread cubes
1 tbs. minced fresh parsley
1 pt. raw oysters with liquid
2 beaten eggs
1 tsp. poultry seasoning
1 tsp. salt
1/8 tsp. black pepper
1/4 cup whole milk

In a skillet over medium heat, add the bay leaf, celery, onion and butter. Saute the vegetables for 4 minutes or until they are tender. Remove the skillet from the heat and discard the bay leaf. Spoon the vegetables and butter into a mixing bowl.

Drain the oysters but save the liquid. Add the bread cubes, parsley, oysters, eggs, poultry seasoning, salt and black pepper to the mixing bowl. Toss until combined. Add the oyster liquid and milk in a small bowl. Add just enough of the liquid to moisten the bread cubes. If the oysters did not have much liquid, add additional milk as needed.

Stuff the turkey or bake the stuffing on the side. To bake the stuffing, preheat the oven to 350°. Spoon the stuffing into a 2 quart casserole dish. Bake for 20-30 minutes or until the stuffing is hot, set and lightly golden. Remove the stuffing from the oven and serve.

Vegetable Stuffing

Makes 6 cups or enough to stuff an 8 lb. turkey

1 cup chopped onion
4 tbs. unsalted butter
1/4 cup minced fresh parsley
2 tbs. pimento stuffed green olives
6 canned water chestnuts, chopped
1/4 cup hot water
4 cups herb seasoned stuffing croutons

In a skillet over medium heat, add the onion and butter. Saute the onion for 5 minutes. Stir in the parsley, green olives, water chestnuts and water. Stir frequently and heat until the mixture boils. Remove the pan from the heat.

Preheat the oven to 350°. Spoon the stuffing croutons in a 2 quart casserole dish. Pour the onion mixture over the croutons. Toss until the croutons are moistened. Spread the stuffing smoothly in the pan. Bake for 20 minutes or until the stuffing is hot. If used to stuff a turkey, do not bake the stuffing.

Pumpernickel Stuffing

Makes 6 servings

1 1/2 cups chopped onions
4 tbs. pan drippings (use drippings from turkey, chicken, duck or goose)
3 cups stale pumpernickel bread, cubed
3 cups stale white bread, cubed
1/2 cup water
1 tsp. salt
1/4 tsp. black pepper
1/4 cup chicken broth, optional

You can substitute melted unsalted butter for the pan drippings if desired. This stuffing is served drier than most stuffing.

In a large skillet over medium heat, add the pan drippings and onions. Saute the onions for 4 minutes. Stir in the pumpernickel bread, white bread, water, salt and black pepper. Toss to combine the ingredients. Add the chicken broth if needed to further moisten the stuffing.

Preheat the oven to 325°. Spoon the stuffing into a 2 quart casserole. Bake until the stuffing is golden brown and crisp.

Cranberry Pecan Stuffing

Makes 12 servings

1 1/2 cups sliced celery
3/4 cup chopped onion
1/3 cup unsalted butter
1 1/2 tsp. dried sage, crushed
3/4 tsp. dried thyme, crushed
1/2 tsp. black pepper
9 cups dry bread crumbs
3/4 cup toasted chopped pecans
3/4 cup dried cranberries
3/4 to 1 cup chicken broth

In a sauce pan over medium heat, add the celery, onion and butter. Stir frequently and saute the onion and celery until they are tender. Remove the pan from the heat and stir in the sage, thyme and black pepper.

In a large mixing bowl, add the bread cubes, celery mixture, pecans and cranberries. Toss until combined. Add 3/4 cup chicken broth and toss until the stuffing is moistened. Add the remaining 1/4 cup broth if needed.

This recipe will stuff a 16 lb. turkey. To bake the stuffing separately, preheat the oven to 325°. Spray a 9 x 13 baking dish with non stick cooking spray. Spoon the stuffing into the dish. Cover the dish with a lid or aluminum foil. Bake for 40-50 minutes. The stuffing should be set and hot.

Apple Walnut Sourdough Stuffing

Makes 12 servings

2 cups chopped celery
1 3/4 cups chopped onion
3/4 tsp. dried sage, crushed
1/2 tsp. salt
1/2 tsp. black pepper
1/4 tsp. dried thyme, crushed
3 tbs. unsalted butter
2 cups chopped apples
4 garlic cloves, minced
9 1/2 cups stale sourdough bread, cubed
3/4 cup raisins
3/4 cup toasted walnuts or pecans
1/4 cup minced fresh parsley
1 1/2 to 2 cups chicken broth

In a large skillet over medium heat, add the butter. When the butter is hot and sizzling, add the celery, onion, sage, salt, black pepper and thyme. Stir frequently and cook for 8-10 minutes. The onion and celery should be tender.

Stir in the apples and garlic. Cook for 3 minutes or until the apples begin to soften. In a large mixing bowl, add the cubed bread. Spoon the ingredients from the skillet over the bread. Add the raisins, walnuts and parsley. Toss until combined. Add 1 1/2 cups chicken broth. Stir gently to moisten the bread. Use the remaining chicken broth if needed.

This will stuff a 14 lb. turkey. To cook the stuffing separately, spoon the stuffing into a 9 x 13 baking pan. Cover the pan with aluminum foil. Preheat the oven to 325°. Bake the stuffing for 30 minutes. Remove the aluminum foil from the stuffing. Bake about 15 minutes or until the top is golden brown.

Pineapple Stuffing

This stuffing is perfect with roast chicken. It makes just the perfect amount to use as a side dish.

Makes 6 servings

1/2 cup unsalted butter, melted
8 oz. can crushed pineapple, drained
3 cups soft bread cubes
1/2 cup sweetened flaked coconut
1/2 cup chopped celery
1/8 tsp. salt

In a mixing bowl, add the pineapple, bread cubes, coconut, salt and celery. Toss to combine the ingredients. Drizzle the melted butter over the bread cubes. Toss until well combined.

Preheat the oven to 325°. Spray a 1 quart casserole dish with non stick cooking spray. Spoon the stuffing into the prepared dish. Bake for 15-20 minutes or until the stuffing is set and lightly golden on top.

Herb Stuffing

Makes about 10 cups or enough to stuff a 14 lb. turkey

1 large onion, chopped
1 cup unsalted butter
1 cup finely chopped celery
2 tsp. granulated chicken bouillon
1 tsp. poultry seasoning
1/2 tsp. salt
1/4 tsp. black pepper
1 1/4 cups water
12 cups cubed white bread
3/4 cup minced fresh parsley

In a sauce pan over medium heat, add the onion, butter and celery. Saute the onion and celery for 4 minutes. Stir in the chicken bouillon, poultry seasoning, salt, black pepper and water. Stir until well combined and bring the liquids to a boil. Remove the pan from the heat.

Preheat the oven to 350°. Spray a 3 quart rectangular casserole dish with non stick cooking spray. In a large mixing bowl, add the bread and parsley. Pour the sauce pan ingredients over the bread. Using a heavy spoon, toss to coat the bread with the liquids.

Spoon the stuffing into the prepared dish. Bake for 30-40 minutes. The stuffing should be set, moist and the top lightly browned. You can use this stuffing inside your turkey if desired. Mix the stuffing only until moist and place in the cavity of your bird.

Mushroom Stuffing

Makes about 10 cups or enough to stuff a 14 lb. turkey

1 lb. fresh mushrooms
1 1/2 cups sliced green onions
1 cup unsalted butter
12 cups bread, cubed
1 tsp. salt

In a skillet over medium heat, add the mushrooms, green onions and butter. Saute the mushrooms and green onions about 10 minutes. The vegetables should be tender. Remove the skillet from the heat.

In a large mixing bowl, add the bread cubes. Add the mushrooms with any liquid to the bowl. Sprinkle the salt over the bread. Toss until well combined and the bread is moistened.

Preheat the oven to 350°. Spray a 3 quart casserole dish with non stick cooking spray. Spoon the stuffing into the casserole dish. Bake for 25-35 minutes or until the stuffing is set and lightly browned.

Do not bake if using the stuffing inside the turkey.

Sausage Apple Stuffing

Makes about 10 cups or enough to stuff a 14 lb. turkey

8 cups cubed bread
1 lb. ground pork sausage roll
1 cup onion, diced
2 apples, peeled, cored and diced
1/2 cup water
1 tsp. salt

Preheat the oven to 250°. Place the bread cubes on a large cookie sheet. Bake for 10 minutes. Baking the bread will help to toast and dry out the bread. You need a dry bread for this recipe. Remove the bread from the oven and let the bread cool while you prepare the rest of the stuffing.

Cut the sausage into 8 thick slices. Place the sausage in a skillet over medium heat. Cook about 5 minutes per side or until the sausage is done and no longer pink. Remove the sausage from the skillet but leave the pan drippings.

Place the sausage and bread in a large mixing bowl. Drain off all but 2 tablespoons of the sausage drippings from the skillet. Add the onion to the skillet and saute the onion for 5 minutes. Stir in the apples, water and salt. Stir until combined and cook until the mixture boils. Remove the pan from the heat and pour the mixture over the bread and sausage. Toss lightly until the bread is slightly moistened.

If you are using the stuffing to stuff a turkey, you can leave the stuffing as it sits. If you want to bake the stuffing separately, add about 1/2 to 1 cup chicken broth to the stuffing if needed to make a moist stuffing.

Spoon the stuffing into a 3 quart casserole dish. Bake for 20-30 minutes. The stuffing should be hot and lightly golden.

Parsley Stuffing

Makes 8 cups or enough to stuff a 10 lb. turkey

12 cups stale bread, cubed
1 1/2 tsp. rubbed sage
1 1/2 tsp. dried thyme
1 1/2 tsp. dried rosemary
1 1/2 tsp. salt
1/3 cup minced fresh parsley
1/3 cup finely chopped onion
1/3 cup melted unsalted butter
1-2 cups chicken broth

Preheat the oven to 350°. In a mixing bowl, add the bread cubes, sage, thyme, rosemary, salt, parsley, onion and melted butter. Toss until combined. Add 1 cup chicken broth. Toss until the bread is moistened. You only want the bread to be moistened. Add the remaining chicken broth if needed.

To bake the stuffing separately, spray a 9 x 13 baking pan with non stick cooking spray. You may need to add additional chicken broth for baking the stuffing. The stuffing needs to be moist but not soupy. Bake for 30-40 minutes or until the stuffing is lightly browned and hot.

Orange Stuffing

Makes 4 servings

3 cups toasted bread, cubed
2 cups finely diced celery
1 tbs. grated orange zest
2/3 cup diced orange sections
3/4 tsp. salt
1/2 tsp. poultry seasoning
1/8 tsp. black pepper
1 egg, beaten
1/4 cup melted unsalted butter
1/4 - 1/2 cup chicken broth

Preheat the oven to 350°. Spray a 2 quart casserole dish with non stick cooking spray. In a mixing bowl, add the bread, celery, orange zest, orange sections, salt, poultry seasoning and black pepper. In a small bowl, add the egg and melted butter. Whisk until well combined.

Pour the butter and egg over the bread cubes. Toss until blended and the bread moistened. Add 1/4 cup chicken broth and toss to moisten the bread. Add the remaining chicken broth if needed.

Spoon the stuffing into the prepared casserole dish. Bake for 30-40 minutes or until the stuffing is hot and set. The top should be lightly browned.

Lemon Herb Stuffing

Makes 4 servings

3 tbs. grated lemon zest
4 tbs. lemon juice
2 cups soft bread crumbs
1 tsp. dried thyme
1/2 tsp. dried marjoram
1/2 tsp. rubbed sage
Salt and black pepper to taste
1 egg, beaten
1/8 - 1/4 cup water

In a small bowl, add the lemon zest, lemon juice, egg and 1/8 cup water. Whisk until well combined. In a large mixing bowl, add the bread crumbs, thyme, marjoram and sage. Toss until well combined. Pour the lemon juice mixture over the bread crumbs. Add the remaining water if needed to moisten the bread crumbs. Season with salt and black pepper.

Preheat the oven to 350°. Spoon the stuffing into a 2 quart casserole dish. Bake for 30-40 minutes or until the stuffing is set and lightly golden.

Bacon and Herb Stuffing

Makes 4 servings

3 slices bacon
1 tbs. unsalted butter
1 cup finely chopped onion
1 1/2 cups soft bread crumbs
2 tbs. minced fresh parsley
1/2 tsp. dried thyme
1/2 tsp. dried basil
Salt and black pepper to taste
1 egg, beaten

In a skillet over medium heat, add the bacon. Cook the bacon for 6-7 minutes or until the bacon is crisp. Remove the bacon from the skillet and drain on paper towels. Crumble the bacon.

Add the butter and onion to the skillet with the bacon drippings. Saute the onion for 4 minutes. Add the bread crumbs, parsley, basil and thyme. Toss until the bread crumbs are moistened. Remove the skillet from the heat and stir in the egg and bacon. Season with salt and black pepper if desired.

Preheat the oven to 350°. Spoon the stuffing into a 2 quart casserole dish. Bake for 30-40 minutes or until the stuffing is set and golden brown.

Brown Rice Stuffing

Makes about 10 cups or enough to stuff a 14 lb. turkey

9 cups water
1 tbs. salt
3 cups brown rice
2 cups chopped celery
1 large onion, diced
1/2 cup unsalted butter
1/2 cup minced fresh parsley
1 1/2 tsp. poultry seasoning
Additional salt to taste

In a large sauce pan over medium heat, add the water and 1 tablespoon salt. Bring the water to a boil. Stir in the rice and reduce the heat to low. Place a lid on the sauce pan and cook about 45 minutes. The rice should be tender. Remove the pan from the heat and drain off any water if needed. Place the rice in a large mixing bowl.

In a skillet over medium heat, add the celery, onion and butter. Saute the onion and celery for 5 minutes. Add the parsley and poultry seasoning. Stir until well combined. Remove the skillet from the heat and pour the mixture over the rice. Toss until combined. Season with additional salt if desired.

Stuff the turkey with the stuffing if desired. For baked stuffing, you may need to add 1/2 to 1 cup chicken broth for extra moisture. The rice should be moist but not soupy.

To bake the stuffing, spray a 3 quart casserole dish with non stick cooking spray. Spoon the rice stuffing into the dish. Preheat the oven to 350°. Bake for 20 minutes or until the stuffing is hot.

Apricot Stuffing

Makes 8 servings

This stuffing is to be served as a side dish. Do not stuff a turkey with this recipe.

1 cup dried apricots, chopped
1 1/2 cups water
1 cup diced celery
1/2 cup unsalted butter
1 tsp. granulated chicken bouillon granules
1 cup chopped pecans
1 tsp. salt
6 cups bread, cubed

In a sauce pan over medium heat, add the apricots and 1/2 cup water. Bring the water to a boil and remove the pan from the heat. Place a lid on the sauce pan and let the apricots sit for 10 minutes.

In a skillet over medium heat, add the celery and butter. Saute the celery for 5 minutes. Stir in the chicken bouillon granules, 1 cup water, pecans and salt. Cook only until the water boils. Remove the pan from the heat.

In a large bowl, add the bread cubes, apricots and the celery mixture. Toss until well combined. Preheat the oven to 350°. Spoon the stuffing into a 2 quart casserole dish. Cover the dish with a lid or aluminum foil. Bake for 50-60 minutes. The stuffing should be hot, moist and set.

Wild Rice Stuffing

Makes 4 cups

6 oz. pkg. long grain and wild rice mix
1/2 cup chopped celery
1/2 cup water chestnuts, chopped
1/2 cup cooked mushrooms, sliced
4 tbs. unsalted butter, melted
1 tbs. soy sauce

Cook the rice according to the package directions. Cool the rice before adding the remaining ingredients.

In a mixing bowl, add the rice, celery, water chestnuts, mushrooms, butter and soy sauce. Stir until well blended. Use the stuffing for Cornish game hens, turkey or chicken.

To serve the stuffing as a side dish, place the rice stuffing in a 2 quart casserole dish. Place a lid on the casserole dish or cover the dish with aluminum foil. Bake at 350° for 20-25 minutes or until the stuffing is hot.

Mock Wild Rice Dressing

Makes 6 cups

1/3 cup unsalted butter
2 cups instant rice, uncooked
1/2 cup chopped onions
3/4 lb. fresh mushrooms, chopped
1 1/2 cups diced celery
1/4 cup chopped celery leaves
1 1/2 tsp. salt
1/4 tsp. dried marjoram
1/8 tsp. black pepper
Pinch of rubbed sage
Pinch of dried thyme
2 cups water
1/2 cup chopped pecans

In a large skillet over medium low heat, add the butter, rice, onions, mushrooms, celery, celery leaves, salt, marjoram, black pepper, sage and thyme. Stir frequently and saute the vegetables for 12-15 minutes. Add the water and bring the mixture to a boil. Cook for 4-5 minutes or until the rice is tender. Remove the skillet from the heat.

Fluff the rice gently with a fork. Add the pecans and gently toss until well combined. Use this as a side dish. The rice will become inedible if used for stuffing a chicken or turkey.

Rice and Corn Dressing

Makes 8 servings

1 cup chopped pecans
2 cups long grain rice, uncooked
2 cups whole kernel corn, cooked
1/2 cup roasted red bell peppers, diced
4 cups chicken broth
1/2 cup chopped celery
1/2 cup chopped green bell pepper
1/2 cup fresh minced parsley
1 cup chopped onion
1/4 cup unsalted butter
Salt and black pepper to taste

In a skillet over medium low heat, add the rice, red bell peppers, celery, green bell pepper, parsley, onion and butter. Saute the rice and vegetables until the vegetables soften and the rice is golden brown.

Add the corn, pecans and chicken broth. Bring the mixture to a boil. Reduce the heat to low. Cover the skillet with a lid. Simmer for 20-30 minutes or until the rice is done and most of the liquid is absorbed. Taste the dish and add salt and black pepper to taste.

This is delicious with barbeque meats or grilled chicken.

Fruity Rice Stuffing

Makes 4 servings

1 cup grated onion
2 tbs. unsalted butter
1 cup cooked rice
1 tbs. chopped raisins
1 tbs. chopped dried apricots
1 tbs. dried currants
1 tbs. pine nuts
1 tbs. grated lemon zest
1 egg, beaten
Salt and black pepper

In a skillet over medium heat, add the onion and butter. Saute the onion for 3 minutes. Stir in the rice, raisins, apricots and currants. Stir constantly and cook for 4 minutes.

Remove the skillet from the heat and stir in the pine nuts, lemon zest and egg. Season with salt and black pepper.

Preheat the oven to 350°. Spoon the stuffing into a 2 quart casserole dish. Bake for 20-25 minutes. The stuffing should be set and hot. The top should be lightly golden brown.

4 SAUCES, GLAZES & GRAVY

In the south, we eat gravy like a vegetable. We would never grill or barbecue meat with a dry rub or marinade.

I have included our favorite gravy, dry rubs or marinades for meats. Try them on your favorite cut of meat. The Pan Drippings Gravy recipe works for any meat. Try these recipes on your holiday turkey or feast.

Maple Pecan Ham Glaze or Sauce

Makes 3 cups

1 1/2 cups maple syrup
1 1/2 cups orange marmalade
2 tbs. unsalted butter
3/4 cup chopped toasted pecans

In a sauce pan over low heat, add the maple syrup and orange marmalade. Stir constantly and cook until the glaze is hot and just begins to bubble. Remove the glaze from the heat and stir in the butter and pecans.

This will glaze a 6 lb. ham. Due to the high sugar content, glaze the ham during the last 15 minutes of baking.

I spread about 1 cup glaze on the ham and serve the warm glaze as a sauce on the side. Don't just save this glaze for ham. It is delicious on pork, chicken, carrots and sweet potatoes.

Cranberry Glaze

Makes 1 3/4 cups

12 oz. can frozen cranberry juice concentrate, thawed
3 tbs. Dijon mustard
2 tbs. light brown sugar
2 tbs. lemon juice
4 tsp. cornstarch
1/4 tsp. ground cloves

In a sauce pan over low heat, add all the ingredients. Stir constantly and cook until the sauce thickens and bubbles. When the sauce boils, cook for 2 additional minutes. Remove the sauce from the heat.

Use the glaze on turkey, chicken, pork, ham or ribs. Baste the meat before cooking and several times during the cooking process.

You can also cool the glaze and use as a marinade. Marinate the meat for 8-12 hours in the refrigerator.

Baked Ham Pineapple Glaze

Makes 1 cup

1/2 cup light brown sugar
1/2 cup unsweetened pineapple juice
1/4 cup white vinegar
1 tsp. yellow prepared mustard

Combine all the ingredients in a bowl. Stir until well combined. Brush on the ham during the last 20 minutes of cooking time.

This glaze has a high sugar content and will burn easily. Do not glaze the ham before baking the ham with the glaze. The glaze will burn. After removing the ham from the oven, you can glaze the ham again before serving.

This glaze is also good on chicken or pork.

Giblet Gravy

This is an old recipe that my mother used every time she roasted a turkey. You can easily substitute chicken giblets for the turkey if desired.

Makes 4 cups

Turkey giblets
1 onion, chopped
1/4 cup celery leaves
1 tsp. salt
1 bay leaf
4 cups water
Turkey liver
8 tbs. turkey fat pan drippings
1/2 cup all purpose flour
Salt and black pepper to taste

In a sauce pan over medium heat, add the giblets, onion, celery leaves, 1 teaspoon salt, bay leaf and water. Bring the gravy to a boil and reduce the heat to low. Simmer for 1 1/2 hours. Add the turkey liver and simmer for 20 minutes. Remove the pan from the heat and strain the broth. Save the giblets and liver from the broth. You need four cups broth. Add water if needed to make 4 cups.

Finely chop the giblets and liver. Add them to the broth. Cool the broth in the refrigerator until you are ready to make the gravy. When you are ready to make the gravy, add 8 tablespoons turkey fat pan drippings to a sauce pan. Place the pan over medium heat. Stir in the all purpose flour. Stir constantly until the mixture bubbles. Stir in the broth, giblets and liver. Stir constantly and cook until the gravy boils. Cook for 1 minute after the gravy boils. Remove the pan from the heat and season to taste with salt and black pepper.

Onion Mushroom Turkey Gravy

Makes 4 cups

Turkey giblets and neck
Turkey liver
1 bay leaf
3 1/2 cups water
1 envelope onion soup mix
8 tbs. turkey fat pan drippings
1/2 cup all purpose flour
1 cup diced cooked mushrooms

In a sauce pan over medium heat, add the turkey giblets and neck, bay leaf and water. Bring the mixture to a boil. Stir in the onion soup mix. Reduce the heat to low and simmer for 40 minutes. Add the turkey liver and simmer for 20 minutes. Remove the pan from the heat.

Strain the broth. Discard the giblets and liver. You need 3 1/2 cups broth. Add water if needed to make 3 1/2 cups. In a sauce pan over medium heat, add the turkey pan drippings and all purpose flour. Stir constantly while making the gravy. Cook for 2 minutes and add the reserved broth and mushrooms. Cook until the sauce boils. Cook for 1 minute after the sauce boils. Remove the pan from the heat and serve.

Pan Drippings Gravy

Use this recipe to make any gravy from pan drippings. Turkey, chicken, sausage, bacon and beef are very good.

Amount varies based upon how much gravy you need.

Pan drippings
Salt and black pepper to taste
All purpose flour
Broth, water or milk
1/4 cup finely chopped cooked meat, optional

Before using the pan drippings, scrape the bottom of the roasting pan to loosen all the bits of food that stick to the pan. You want a few of the food bits left in the pan in the gravy.

For each cup of gravy, add 2 tablespoons pan drippings to a sauce pan over medium heat. Stir in 2 tablespoons all purpose flour. Season to taste with salt and black pepper. Stir constantly while making the gravy. I like to use a whisk since it makes a smoother gravy. Cook the flour and pan drippings until the flour begins to brown.

Add 1 cup broth, milk or water for each cup of gravy. Cook until the gravy thickens and bubbles. Remove the gravy from the heat. Taste the gravy and season with salt and black pepper if needed.

Add the meat of your choice to the gravy if desired. Use cooked chicken for chicken gravy, cooked turkey for turkey gravy and cooked beef for beef gravy. The meat is optional but it does add great flavor to the gravy.

I like to use chicken broth for chicken gravy. Beef broth for beef gravy and turkey broth for turkey gravy. A mixture of half broth and half milk is also good. You can add a few drops kitchen bouquet or any browning gravy sauce if desired.

A drop or two of Worcestershire sauce is also good.

Easy and Quick Canned Soup Gravy

This recipe can make a multitude of gravies. Vary the canned soups to make any flavor you need.

3 tbs. pan drippings
1/4 cup water
10.75 oz can cream soup (use your favorite flavor)
1/4 cup cooked meat or vegetables, finely chopped

If you want chicken gravy, use cream of chicken soup. For mushroom gravy, use cream of mushroom soup. For a savory gravy, use cream of celery soup. A broccoli gravy is good over chicken and pork chops. Use a can of cream of broccoli soup for broccoli gravy.

Scrape the bottom of the roasting pan to remove all the bits of food stuck to the pan. Place 3 tablespoons pan drippings in a sauce pan over medium heat. When the pan drippings are hot, stir in the water and canned cream soup. Stir constantly and cook until the gravy thickens and bubbles. Thin with additional water if desired.

Add the meat or vegetable of your choice to the gravy if desired. Use cooked chicken for chicken gravy, cooked turkey for turkey gravy and cooked beef for beef gravy. The meat and vegetables are optional but it does add great flavor to the gravy.

Don't just save these gravies for the holidays. Use the same gravy recipes for meat and vegetable pot pies. Serve the gravies over biscuits or rolls.

Duck Gravy

Makes 2 1/2 cups gravy

4 tbs. pan drippings from a roasted duck
4 tbs. all purpose flour
2 cups chicken broth
1/4 cup finely chopped cooked duck
Salt and black pepper to taste

Scrape the pan from roasting the duck to remove all the food bits on the bottom of the pan. In a sauce pan over medium heat, add the pan drippings. When the pan drippings are hot, stir in the all purpose flour. Stir constantly while making the gravy. Cook until the flour just begins to brown. Add the chicken broth and cooked duck. Cook until the gravy thickens and bubbles. Cook for 1 minute after the gravy boils.

Remove the pan from the heat and season to taste with salt and black pepper.

Garlic Oregano Meat Marinade

Makes about 1 1/3 cups marinade

3/4 cup vegetable oil
1/2 cup vinegar
1 tbs. dried oregano
1/4 tsp. salt
1/4 tsp. black pepper
2 garlic cloves, minced

Combine all the ingredients. Pour over 2 lbs. chicken, beef or pork. Marinate for 8 hours. Discard unused marinade.

Smoky Brisket Sauce

Makes 3 cups

1 1/2 cups apple cider vinegar
1 cup ketchup
1/2 cup light brown sugar
1/4 cup Worcestershire sauce
2 tbs. unsalted butter
1/2 tbs. onion powder
1/2 tbs. garlic powder
1/2 tbs. ground cumin
1 tsp. salt
1/2 tsp. black pepper
1/2 tsp. cayenne pepper

In a sauce pan over medium heat, add all the ingredients. Bring the sauce to a boil. Stir to combine the ingredients. Remove the pan from the heat and let the sauce cool for 45 minutes.

If baking a brisket in the oven or crock pot, pour the sauce over the brisket. Baste several times during the cooking process.

To grill the brisket, pour the sauce over the brisket. Marinate the brisket for 3 hours in the refrigerator. Remove the brisket from the marinade and grill over slow coals for 5-7 hours. Brush the leftover marinade over the brisket during the last 30 minutes of cooking.

Spicy Pork Dry Rub

Makes 3 cups

1 cup light brown sugar
1/2 cup garlic powder
1/2 cup paprika
1/2 cup salt
2 tbs. onion powder
2 tbs. cayenne pepper
2 tbs. chipotle powder
2 tbs. sweet ancho powder
1 tbs. chili powder
1 tbs. ground cumin
1 tbs. black pepper
1 tbs. dry mustard

Combine all the ingredients in a mixing bowl. Sprinkle over any cut of pork. Cook as desired.

Beef Dry Rub

Makes 2 cups

3/4 cup paprika
1/4 cup black pepper
1/4 cup salt
1/4 cup granulated sugar
2 tbs. chili powder
2 tbs. garlic powder
2 tbs. garlic salt
2 tbs. onion powder
2 tsp. cayenne pepper

Combine all the ingredients in a small bowl. Sprinkle to season over any cut of beef. Cook as desired.

Seafood Cajun Dry Rub

Makes 1/2 cup

2 tbs. paprika
2 tsp. cayenne pepper
1 tbs. salt
1 tbs. black pepper
1 tbs. garlic powder
2 tbs. onion powder
1 tsp. dried oregano
1 tbs. dried thyme

Combine all ingredients in a small bowl. Sprinkle to season over any seafood. Cook as desired.

Barbecue Sauce

My husband received this sauce in a mason jar one year for a gift. It was in a nice basket with grilling spices, apron and grilling tools. We loved the sauce so much, we had to get the recipe.

Makes about 3 1/2 cups

1/3 cup chopped onion
1 1/2 cups ketchup
1/4 cup apple cider vinegar
1/4 cup steak sauce
1 tsp. liquid smoke
1/2 tsp. cayenne pepper
2 tbs. prepared horseradish
1 tbs. vegetable oil
1/2 cup chili sauce
1/4 cup molasses
3 tbs. dry mustard
1 tsp. garlic powder
1/4 tsp. ground allspice
1 tsp. lemon juice

In a sauce pan over medium heat, add the vegetable oil and onion. Saute the onion for 4 minutes. Add the remaining ingredients. Stir until well combined. Reduce the heat to low. Simmer for 20 minutes. Store in an airtight jar in the refrigerator.

Use this sauce on any meat.

Wine Mushroom Butter

This is divine over cooked steaks or any piece of cooked beef.

Makes about 2 1/2 cups

1 cup unsalted butter, softened
1/3 cup finely chopped onion
1/2 cup portobello mushrooms, finely chopped
1 tsp. minced garlic
1/2 cup red wine
2 tbs. minced fresh parsley
1 tsp. black pepper
1 tsp. salt

In a sauce pan over medium heat, add 1 tablespoon butter and the onion. Saute the onion for 3 minutes. Add the mushrooms and garlic. Saute the mushrooms for 7 minutes. Add the wine and simmer for 4 minutes.

Remove the pan from the heat and cool completely. Once the mixture is cool, stir in the remaining softened butter, parsley, black pepper and salt. Use immediately over any cooked beef or store in the refrigerator no more than 4 days.

5 SIDE DISHES

Holiday dinners require many side dishes. Side dishes are a must for potlucks, picnics and barbecues.

Included are our family favorite side dishes. These recipes are not just for holidays. Use them for dinner meals too.

Included are recipes for squash, potato, sweet potato, green beans, corn, tomatoes, carrots, peas, beans, greens and salads.

Baked Stuffed Yellow Squash

Makes 4-6 servings

3 medium yellow squash
1/4 lb. ground pork sausage
1/4 cup uncooked long grain rice
1 medium onion, chopped
2 tsp. dried parsley
Salt and pepper to taste
8 tbs. unsalted butter
6 tbs. crushed cracker or potato chip crumbs

In a saucepan, add the rice and enough water to cover the rice. Place the sauce pan over medium heat. Bring the rice to a boil. Reduce the heat to low. Place a lid on the pan and cook until the rice is tender or about 25 minutes. Drain the rice and set aside. Add the sausage to a skillet over medium heat. Stir frequently to break the sausage into crumbles as it cooks. Cooks for 7-8 minutes or until the sausage is done. Drain the sausage. Add the cooked rice to the sausage in the skillet.

In a saucepan, place the whole yellow squash and cover the squash with water. Boil the squash for 10 minutes or until the outside of the squash are tender. Remove the pan from the heat and drain all the water from the squash. Cool the squash for 10 minutes.

When the squash are cool, cut the squash in half. Remove the center portion of the squash leaving about a 1/2" thick shell. Add the removed squash to the rice and sausage in the skillet. Add the chopped onion, 2 tablespoons butter and the dried parsley to the skillet. Stir until well combined. Taste the mixture and season with salt and pepper to taste.

Preheat your oven to 375°. Place the squash shells on a baking sheet. Distribute the sausage rice mixture evenly among the six squash shells. Sprinkle one tablespoon of the cracker or potato chip crumbs on top of the sausage rice mixture in the squash. Dot each squash with one tablespoon of butter. Bake for 30 minutes or until the top is golden brown and the sausage rice mixture is hot.

Cheddar Squash Bake

Makes 8 servings

6 cups unpeeled zucchini, thinly sliced
1 tbs. salt
2 beaten egg yolks
1 cup sour cream
2 tbs. all purpose flour
2 egg whites, stiffly beaten
6 slices cooked bacon, crumbled
3/4 cup shredded cheddar cheese
1 tbs. unsalted butter, melted
1/4 cup dry bread crumbs

Preheat the oven to 350°. Place the zucchini in a mixing bowl. Sprinkle the salt over the zucchini. In a mixing bowl, add the egg yolks, sour cream and all purpose flour. Stir until well blended. Gently fold in the stiffly beaten egg whites.

Place 1/2 of the zucchini in a 10 x 8 baking dish. Spoon half of the egg mixture over the zucchini. Place the remaining zucchini on top of the egg mixture. Spoon the remaining egg mixture over the zucchini.

Sprinkle the cheddar cheese and bacon over the top of the zucchini. Sprinkle the bread crumbs over the cheese. Drizzle the melted butter over the bread crumbs. Bake for 20-25 minutes or until the zucchini are tender and the casserole hot.

Fruit Filled Acorn Squash

Makes 6 servings

3 medium acorn squash, halved and seeded
1/2 tsp. salt
3 cups chopped apple
1 orange, peeled and diced
1/2 cup light brown sugar
1/4 cup unsalted butter, melted

Preheat the oven to 350°. Place the squash on a baking pan with the cut side down. Bake for 35 minutes. Remove the pan from the oven and turn the squash over so the cut side is up. Sprinkle the squash with salt.

In a mixing bowl, add the apple, orange, brown sugar and melted butter. Stir until well combined. Spoon the fruit mixture into the center of each squash. Bake for 25 minutes or until the squash and apple are tender. Remove the squash from the oven and cool for 5 minutes before serving.

Candied Butternut Squash

Makes 8 servings

2 butternut squash, about 1 1/2 lbs. each
1/2 cup light brown sugar
3 tbs. molasses
3 tbs. unsalted butter, melted
1 tsp. orange peel, shredded
1/2 tsp. ground cinnamon
1/4 tsp. ground cloves

Preheat the oven to 350°. Cut the squash into quarters. Remove the seeds. Place the squash, cut side down, on a large baking pan. Cover the squash with aluminum foil. Bake for 40 minutes.

In a small bowl, add the brown sugar, molasses, butter, orange peel, cinnamon and cloves. Stir to combine.

Remove the squash from the oven and turn the squash with the peel side down. Spoon the sauce over the squash. Leave off the aluminum foil and bake the squash for 20 minutes.

Mama's Squash Casserole

Makes 6 servings

2 cups cooked yellow squash, drained
1 cup whole milk
2 eggs, beaten
1/2 cup unsalted butter
1/2 tsp. salt
1/2 tsp. black pepper
1 onion, chopped
1 green bell pepper, chopped
1 cup crushed cracker crumbs

Preheat the oven to 350°. In a skillet over medium heat, add the butter, onion and green bell pepper. Saute the onion and green bell pepper for 3 minutes. Add the squash, milk, eggs, salt and black pepper to the skillet. Mash the squash slightly with a spatula. Cook for 2 minutes.

Spray a 1 1/2 quart casserole with non stick cooking spray. Spoon the squash mixture into the casserole dish. Sprinkle the cracker crumbs across the top. Bake for 50-60 minutes or until slightly golden on top and the casserole is hot.

Lemon Parsley Carrots

Makes 8 servings

4 tbs. unsalted butter
6 cups carrots, sliced and cooked
1 tsp. granulated sugar
1 tsp. salt
2 tbs. lemon juice
2 tbs. fresh minced parsley

In a large sauce pan over medium heat, add the butter. When the butter melts, add the carrots, granulated sugar, salt and lemon juice. Toss to coat the carrots with the sauce.

Cook for 3-4 minutes or until the carrots are heated through. Remove the pan from the heat and spoon the carrots into a serving bowl. Sprinkle the fresh parsley over the carrots.

Carrots Au Gratin

Makes 8 servings

1/4 cup unsalted butter, melted
1 cup chopped onion
1/4 cup all purpose flour
1 tsp. salt
1/4 tsp. black pepper
2 cups whole milk
4 cups sliced carrots, cooked
6 slices American cheese
1 cup buttered bread crumbs

Preheat the oven to 350°. In a skillet over medium heat, add the butter and onion. Saute the onion for 3 minutes. Stir in the all purpose flour, salt and black pepper. Cook for 2 minutes. Slowly add the milk and stir until the sauce begins to thicken. Remove the pan from the heat to assemble the casserole.

Spray a 2 quart casserole dish with non stick cooking spray. Place 2 cups of the carrots in the casserole dish. Place 3 slices cheese over the carrots. Pour 1/2 of the sauce over the cheese and carrots. Repeat with the remaining carrots, cheese and sauce. Top the casserole with the buttered bread crumbs.

Bake for 35-40 minutes or until the top is lightly browned and the casserole is hot.

Note: This casserole can be made ahead of time. Do not add the bread crumbs until you are ready to cook the casserole. It can be refrigerated up to 24 hours before baking. Bake for 50-60 minutes if made ahead.

Orange Baby Carrots

Makes 6 servings

1 lb. baby carrots or about 3 1/2 cups
1 cup orange juice
1/4 cup light brown sugar
1/4 tsp. ground cinnamon

In a sauce pan over medium heat, add the carrots. Cover the carrots with water. Simmer the carrots about 12-15 minutes or until the carrots are tender. Remove the carrots from the heat and drain all the water from the carrots.

Reduce the heat to low. Add the orange juice, brown sugar and cinnamon to the carrots. Stir until the ingredients are well combined. Simmer for 7-8 minutes or until the glaze is well coated on the carrots.

Maple Apple Carrots

Makes 6 servings

3/4 cup sliced onion
3 tbs. unsalted butter
6 carrots, peeled and sliced
2 tbs. maple syrup
1/2 tsp. salt
2 apples, cut into wedges

In a skillet over low heat, add the butter and onion. Saute the onion for 5 minutes. Add the carrots, maple syrup and salt. Stir until the ingredients are well combined. Place a lid on the skillet and simmer for 15 minutes. Stir frequently to keep the carrots and syrup from burning.

Add the apples and place the lid back on the skillet. Cook about 15 minutes or until the carrots and apples are tender.

Corn Custard Casserole

Makes 6 servings

10.75 oz. can cream of celery soup
2 tbs. all purpose flour
1 tbs. yellow prepared mustard
1 1/2 cups cooked whole kernel corn
2/3 cup evaporated milk
2 tbs. chopped green bell pepper
2 tbs. chopped onion
2 tbs. chopped red pimento
1 tsp. Worcestershire sauce

Preheat the oven to 350°. Spray a 11 x 7 casserole dish with non stick cooking spray. In a mixing bowl, add the cream of celery soup, all purpose flour, mustard, corn, milk, green bell pepper, onion, red pimento and Worcestershire sauce. Stir until well combined.

Spoon the mixture into the prepared casserole dish. Bake for 30-40 minutes or until a knife inserted off center of the dish comes out clean. Remove the dish from the oven and let the casserole cool for 5 minutes.

Barbecue Corn

Makes 6 servings

6 ears fresh corn
1/2 cup unsalted butter
3 tbs. bottle barbecue sauce
1/2 tsp. salt
1/4 tsp. black pepper

Husk the corn and remove the silk from each ear of corn. Place each ear of corn on a heavy duty piece of aluminum foil. The aluminum foil needs to be large enough to wrap the corn.

In a small sauce pan over low heat, add the butter, barbecue sauce, salt and black pepper. Stir until the butter melts and the sauce is hot. Remove the pan from the heat.

Brush the sauce on the corn. Wrap the corn in aluminum foil. Bake or grill as desired.

To grill the corn, place the wrapped corn over hot coals. Turn frequently and cook for 15-20 minutes or until the corn is tender.

To bake the corn, place the wrapped corn on a baking sheet. Preheat the oven to 400°. Turn the corn frequently and bake about 20-25 minutes or until the corn is tender.

Grilled Corn

Makes 4 servings

4 ears corn on the cob, shucked and cleaned
1/4 cup unsalted butter, softened
2 tbs. grated Parmesan cheese
1 tsp. minced fresh parsley
1/4 tsp. black pepper

Wrap the corn in aluminum foil. Grill over medium heat for 20-30 minutes or until the corn is tender. Turn the corn frequently for even cooking.

While the corn is grilling, add the butter, Parmesan cheese, parsley and black pepper to a small bowl. Stir until well combined. Spread over hot cooked corn before serving.

Easy Baked Beans

Makes 6 servings

3 cups canned baked beans
1 cup seasoned tomato sauce
1 cup chopped onion
1/4 cup light brown sugar
2 tbs. yellow prepared mustard
1 tsp. salt
4 drops Tabasco sauce
6 slices cooked bacon

Use packaged precooked bacon if desired. Preheat the oven to 300°. Spray a 2 quart casserole dish with non stick cooking spray. Add the baked beans, tomato sauce, onion, brown sugar, mustard, salt and Tabasco sauce to the casserole dish.

Stir until well combined. Cut the bacon into bite size pieces. Stir the bacon into the beans. Bake for 3 hours. Remove the dish from the oven and serve.

To cook this in a crock pot, add the all the ingredients and stir. Set the crock pot on high. Cook for 4 hours. You can set the crock pot on low and cook for 6 hours.

Basil Tomatoes

Makes 8 servings

4 large fresh tomatoes, cut in half lengthwise
4 tbs. unsalted butter
1 tsp. dried basil, crushed
1/4 tsp. dried oregano, crushed
1/4 tsp. garlic salt

Arrange the tomatoes, cut side up, in a 9" square baking pan. In a small bowl, melt the butter in the microwave. Remove the butter when melted and stir in the basil, oregano and garlic salt.

Brush the butter over the tomatoes. Preheat the oven to the broiler position. Broil for 2-3 minutes or until the butter is browned and bubbly.

Marinated Tomatoes

Makes 8 servings

4 large ripe tomatoes, sliced and peeled
1 tbs. lemon juice
1/2 tsp. salt
1/4 cup vegetable oil
1/2 tsp. minced garlic
1/2 tsp. dried oregano, crushed

Place the tomatoes in a large bowl. In a small bowl, add the lemon juice, salt, vegetable oil, garlic and oregano. Stir until well combined. Pour the dressing over the tomatoes. Cover the bowl with a lid or plastic wrap. Chill for 3 hours before serving.

They are delicious in a salad, served by themselves or placed on sandwiches.

Tomato Onion Salad

Makes 8 servings

5 cups diced fresh tomatoes
1 cup finely chopped onion
1/3 cup minced fresh mint
3 tbs. lemon juice
Salt to taste

In a serving bowl, add the tomatoes, onion, mint and lemon juice. Toss until well combined. Cover the bowl and refrigerate for 2 hours before serving. Season with salt to taste.

Grilled Tomatoes in Foil

Makes 4 servings

4 large firm ripe tomatoes
2 tbs. unsalted butter, cut into small pieces
Salt and black pepper to taste
2 tbs. grated Romano cheese

Cut each tomato in half lengthwise. Place the butter pieces on the tomatoes. Sprinkle the tomatoes with salt and black pepper to taste. Sprinkle the Romano cheese over the tomatoes. Place the tomatoes on a large piece of aluminum foil.

Roll the foil to make a packet. Place the packet on the grill and cook for 15-20 minutes or until the tomatoes are hot and the butter and cheese melted.

Lemon Green Beans

Makes 6 servings

1 1/2 lbs. fresh green beans
3 tbs. melted unsalted butter
1/2 tsp. salt
1/4 tsp. black pepper
1 tbs. minced fresh parsley
3 tbs. lemon juice

Trim the ends from the green beans. Cut the green beans into 1 1/2" pieces. Add the green beans to a sauce pan. Cover the green beans with water and place over medium heat. Bring the green beans to a boil. Place a lid on the green beans and simmer about 12-15 minutes or until the green beans are tender. Remove the pan from the heat and drain all the water from the green beans.

Add the butter, salt, black pepper, parsley and lemon juice to the green beans. Toss to coat the green beans with the butter and seasonings.

Scalloped Green Beans

Makes 6 servings

4 slices bacon
1 large onion, chopped
1 cup celery, chopped
1 green bell pepper, chopped
4 cups cooked green beans
1 cup shredded American cheese
3 cups canned or fresh tomatoes, diced
Salt and black pepper to taste

In a skillet over medium heat, add the bacon. Fry the bacon until crisp. Remove the bacon from the skillet but leave the bacon drippings. Drain the bacon on paper towels. Crumble the bacon into pieces.

Reduce the heat in the skillet to low. Add the onion, celery, green bell pepper and tomatoes. Simmer the vegetables for 30 minutes. Remove the skillet from the heat.

Preheat the oven to 350°. In a 2 quart casserole dish, add the green beans. Sprinkle the cheese over the green beans. Add the vegetables from the skillet. Stir until well combined. Season to taste with salt and black pepper. Sprinkle the bacon across the top of the casserole. Bake for 30 minutes or until the dish is hot and the cheese melted.

Vegetable Casserole

Makes 6 servings

1 1/2 cups sliced carrots
1 onion, sliced
10 oz. pkg. frozen spinach, thawed and cooked
3 tbs. unsalted butter
3 tbs. all purpose flour
1 1/2 cups whole milk
1 cup shredded American cheese
1/4 tsp. salt
1/8 tsp. black pepper
1/2 cup buttered bread crumbs

In a sauce pan over medium heat, add the carrots and onion. Cover the carrots with water. Bring the carrots to a boil and cook for 8 minutes. The carrots should be almost tender. Remove the pan from the heat and drain all the water from the pan.

In a sauce pan over medium low heat, add the butter. When the butter melts, stir in the all purpose flour. Stir constantly while making the sauce. Cook until the flour just begins to brown. Stir in the milk, salt and black pepper. Cook until the sauce thickens and bubbles. Remove the pan from the heat and stir in the American cheese. Stir until the cheese melts.

Preheat the oven to 350°. Place half the spinach in a 1 quart casserole dish. Spoon half of the carrots and onion over the spinach. Spread half of the cheese sauce over the carrots and onion. Repeat the layering process using the remaining spinach, carrots and onion and cheese sauce. Sprinkle the bread crumbs over the top. Bake for 20 minutes. The casserole should be hot, bubbly and the top golden brown. Remove the casserole from the oven and serve.

Sweet Caramelized Potatoes

Makes 8 servings

8 potatoes, peeled
1/4 cup granulated sugar
4 tbs. unsalted butter
2 tsp. grated orange rind
1 tsp. salt

Leave the potatoes whole. In a sauce pan over medium heat, add the potatoes and sprinkle the salt over the potatoes. Cover the potatoes with water. Cook the potatoes about 20-25 minutes or until the whole potatoes are tender. Drain the water from the potatoes and keep them warm until the rest of the recipe is ready.

In a heavy skillet or cast iron skillet over medium heat, add the granulated sugar. Stir constantly and cook until the sugar melts and turns golden brown like syrup. Remove the pan from the heat and add the butter. Stir until the butter melts.

Add the potatoes and roll the potatoes in the sugar syrup until they are well coated. Remove the potatoes from the skillet and sprinkle the grated orange rind over the potatoes. You can also substitute sweet potatoes for the white or red potatoes if desired.

Marshmallow Whipped Sweet Potatoes

Makes 8 servings

4 cups hot mashed sweet potatoes
1/4 cup orange juice
3/4 cup light brown sugar
2 cups miniature marshmallows
1/4 cup unsalted butter
1/2 tsp. salt

Preheat the oven to 350°. Spray a 1 1/2 quart casserole dish with non stick cooking spray. In a large bowl, stir together the sweet potatoes, orange juice, brown sugar, 1 cup miniature marshmallows, butter and salt.

Spoon the mixture into the prepared dish. Bake for 20 minutes. Sprinkle the remaining marshmallows over the top. Bake for 5 minutes. Remove the sweet potatoes from the oven and serve.

You can make the casserole ahead of time and refrigerate until ready to bake. Add 15-20 minutes additional baking time if refrigerated.

Sweet Potato Balls

Makes 4 servings

2 1/2 cups mashed hot sweet potatoes
3/4 tsp. salt
1/8 tsp. black pepper
4 tbs. melted unsalted butter
3/4 cup miniature marshmallows
1/3 cup honey
1 cup chopped walnuts

In a mixing bowl, add the sweet potatoes, 2 tablespoons butter, salt, black pepper and marshmallows. Stir until combined. Cover the bowl and refrigerate until well chilled.

Preheat the oven to 350°. Spray a 2 quart baking dish with non stick cooking spray. When the sweet potatoes are chilled, make the balls. Use about 1 tablespoon sweet potatoes and form into a ball. Place the sweet potato balls on a sheet of waxed paper.

In a microwavable bowl, add 1 tablespoon butter and honey. Heat only until the honey is warm and melted. Stir until combined. Using a fork, gently roll the sweet potato balls in the honey butter. In a separate bowl, add the walnuts. Roll the sweet potato balls in the walnuts.

Place the rolled sweet potato balls in the baking dish. Drizzle 1 tablespoon melted butter over the sweet potato balls. Bake for 20 minutes. Remove the dish from the oven and serve.

Summer Garden Potato Salad

Makes 6 servings

6 large potatoes, peeled, cubed and cooked
3 hard boiled eggs, chopped
3/4 cup dill pickles, chopped
3/4 cup sliced radishes
1/2 cup green onions, chopped
1 tsp. salt
1/4 tsp. black pepper
1 1/4 cups mayonnaise

The potatoes need to be cool before using in this recipe. If you cooked the potatoes in water, drain all the water from the potatoes. Chill the cooked potatoes.

In a mixing bowl, add the potatoes, eggs, dill pickles, radishes, green onions, salt, black pepper and mayonnaise. Toss to combine the ingredients. Use additional mayonnaise if desired. Season to taste with additional salt and black pepper. Chill the potato salad at least 2 hours before serving.

Baby Barbecued Potatoes

Makes 6 servings

1 1/2 lbs. baby new potatoes or about 20 new potatoes
2 tbs. olive oil
2 tbs. fresh thyme
1 tsp. sea salt
1 tsp. dry barbecue seasoning

Wash the potatoes thoroughly. In a sauce pan over medium heat, add the potatoes. Cover the potatoes with water and simmer for 12-15 minutes or until the potatoes are tender. Remove the potatoes from the heat and drain all the water from the potatoes.

In a skillet, add the olive oil, thyme and barbecue seasoning. Stir until well combined. Add the potatoes and place the potatoes on a grill or over medium heat on the stove. Stir frequently and toss the potatoes with the olive oil and seasonings. Cook about 15 minutes or until the potatoes are golden brown. Sprinkle the potatoes with sea salt and serve.

Mushroom Scalloped Potatoes

Makes 6 servings

10.75 oz. can cream of mushroom soup
1 cup diced cooked mushrooms
3/4 cup shredded American cheese
1/4 cup diced red pimento
1/2 tsp. salt
2/3 cup evaporated milk
5 cups sliced and peeled potatoes or about 3 large potatoes
1 tsp. paprika or to taste

Preheat the oven to 350°. Spray a 2 quart casserole dish with non stick cooking spray. Place the potatoes in the casserole dish. In a mixing bowl, add the cream of mushroom soup, mushrooms, 1/2 cup American cheese, red pimento, salt and evaporated milk. Stir until well combined.

Spoon the soup mixture over the potatoes. Bake for 45-50 minutes or until the potatoes are tender. Sprinkle the remaining cheese over the potatoes and bake for 5 minutes. Sprinkle the paprika over the casserole before serving.

If you do not like a strong paprika taste, use the paprika to your taste or omit the paprika. You can sprinkle the casserole with black pepper if desired.

Homemade Scalloped Potatoes

Makes 6 servings

4 cups potatoes, thinly sliced
2 tbs. all purpose flour
1 tsp. salt
1/2 tsp. black pepper
3 tbs. unsalted butter, cut into small pieces
2 cups warm whole milk
1/2 cup shredded cheddar cheese

Preheat the oven to 375°. Spray a 2 quart casserole dish with non stick cooking spray. Place one third of the potatoes in the bottom of the dish. In a small bowl, add the all purpose flour, salt and black pepper. Stir until well combined.

Sprinkle 1/2 of the flour mixture over the potatoes. Place another third of the potatoes in the dish. Sprinkle the remaining flour mixture over the potatoes. Place the final layer of potatoes in the dish. Place the butter slices over the top of the potatoes.

Pour the warm milk over the potatoes. Place a lid on the dish or cover the dish with aluminum foil. Bake for 45 minutes. Remove the cover and sprinkle the cheese across the top of the potatoes. Bake for 15 minutes or until the cheese is melted and the potatoes tender.

Sour Cream Potato Salad

Makes 8 servings

4 medium potatoes, cooked
1 cup chopped celery
1/2 cup chopped cucumber
1/4 cup chopped onion
1 1/2 tsp. salt
1 tsp. celery seeds
1/2 tsp. black pepper
1 cup sour cream
1 tbs. yellow prepared mustard
1/2 cup mayonnaise
1 tbs. white vinegar
3 hard boiled eggs

Chill the potatoes and dice them into cubes. In a large bowl, add the potatoes, celery, cucumber, onion, salt, celery seeds and black pepper.

In a small bowl, add the sour cream, mustard, mayonnaise, white vinegar and the yolks from 2 of the hard boiled eggs. Mash the 2 egg yolks into the dressing. Stir until well blended.

Dice the egg whites of 2 hard boiled eggs and add to the potatoes in the bowl. Add the dressing and stir to combine the ingredients. Chill completely before serving or at least 4 hours. Slice the remaining hard boiled egg and place on top of the potato salad as a garnish.

Amaretto Sweet Potatoes

Makes 8 servings

8 large sweet potatoes, peeled and cooked
1/2 cup light brown sugar
2 tbs. orange juice
1/2 cup Amaretto
1/2 cup granulated sugar
1/2 cup melted unsalted butter
2 tsp. grated orange rind
1 cup miniature marshmallows

Preheat the oven to 350°. Mash the sweet potatoes in a mixing bowl until they are smooth with a mixer or a potato masher. Add the brown sugar, orange juice, Amaretto, granulated sugar, butter and orange rind. Stir until well combined.

Spray a 3 quart casserole dish with non stick cooking spray. Spoon the sweet potatoes into the casserole dish. Bake for 20 minutes. The sweet potatoes should be hot. Sprinkle the marshmallows over the top of the sweet potatoes. Bake for 15 minutes or until the marshmallows are melted and lightly toasted.

Maple Syrup Sweet Potatoes

Makes 4 servings

4 medium sweet potatoes
1 cup maple syrup
3 tbs. unsalted butter
2 tbs. whole milk
1/8 tsp. ground cinnamon
1 1/2 tsp. salt

Scrub the sweet potatoes. Add the sweet potatoes to a sauce pan. Sprinkle the potatoes with 1 teaspoon salt. Cover the potatoes with water. Bring the potatoes to a boil and cook about 30-35 minutes or until the potatoes are tender. Remove the pan from the heat and drain all the water from the potatoes. Let the potatoes cool for 10 minutes.

Remove the skin from the potatoes. Place the potatoes in a bowl and mash the sweet potatoes until they are mostly smooth. Preheat the oven to 400°. Add 1/4 cup maple syrup, milk, 1/2 teaspoon salt and cinnamon to the mashed potatoes. Stir until well combined.

Spray a 1 quart casserole with non stick cooking spray. Spoon the sweet potatoes into the casserole dish. In a microwavable bowl, add the remaining syrup and butter. Microwave for 1 minute or until the butter melts. Stir to combine the syrup and butter. Drizzle the syrup and butter over the sweet potatoes. Using a knife, swirl the syrup through the potatoes. The syrup will not be combined and that is what you want. Bake for 20 minutes or until the dish is hot.

Coconut Sweet Potato Bake

Makes 6 servings

3 cups mashed cooked sweet potatoes
1 cup granulated sugar
2 eggs, beaten
1 cup whole milk
1/2 cup sweetened flaked coconut
1/4 tsp. ground nutmeg
1/2 tsp. ground cinnamon
1/2 cup unsalted butter, softened
1/2 cup light brown sugar
1/2 cup chopped pecans

Preheat the oven to 350°. Spray a 2 quart casserole dish with non stick cooking spray. Add the sweet potatoes, granulated sugar, eggs, milk, coconut, nutmeg and cinnamon. Stir until well combined. Spread the mixture evenly in the baking dish. Bake for 30 minutes.

In a small bowl, add the butter, brown sugar and pecans. Stir until well combined. Drop the mixture by teaspoonfuls over the sweet potatoes. Bake for 15 minutes. Remove the dish from the oven and serve.

Candied Sweet Potatoes

Makes 4 servings

2 large sweet potatoes, cut into large chunks
1 tbs. baking soda
3/4 cup granulated sugar
1/2 cup water
1/4 tsp. salt
1/2 orange, thinly sliced
3 tbs. unsalted butter

In a large mixing bowl, add the sweet potatoes. Sprinkle the baking soda over the potatoes. Cover the potatoes with warm water. Let the potatoes soak for 10 minutes. Drain the water from the potatoes.

In a sauce pan over medium heat, add the granulated sugar, water, salt and orange slices. Stir constantly and bring the syrup to a boil. Reduce the heat to low. Add the sweet potatoes and cook until the sweet potatoes are tender. Remove the pan from the heat and stir in the butter.

Brussel Sprouts with Bacon

Makes 8 servings

1 1/4 lbs. fresh brussel sprouts
3 slices thick slab bacon, diced
1/2 tsp. dried thyme
1/4 tsp. salt
1/4 tsp. black pepper

Trim the brussel sprouts and discard any colored leaves. If your brussel sprouts are large, cut them in half. In a sauce pan over medium heat, add the brussel sprouts. Cover the brussel sprouts with water and cook for 8-10 minutes or until tender. Drain the brussel sprouts. Dry the brussel sprouts with paper towels and set aside.

In a large skillet over medium heat, add the bacon. Cook for 6-8 minutes or until the bacon is cooked and crisp. Drain the bacon grease from the pan. Add the brussel sprouts, salt, thyme and black pepper. Cook for 3 minutes or until the brussel sprouts are hot.

Spinach Au Gratin

Makes 4 servings

1 lb. fresh spinach
4 slices bacon
2 tbs. all purpose flour
1 cup whole milk
1/2 cup shredded cheddar cheese
1/2 cup bread crumbs

Wash the spinach thoroughly. Chop the spinach leaves. Place the spinach in a sauce pan over medium heat. You should still have water on the spinach leaves so do not add water to the sauce pan. Cover the sauce pan with a lid and cook for 5 minutes or until the spinach is tender.

In a skillet over medium heat, add the bacon. Cook the bacon until crisp. Remove the bacon from the pan but leave the bacon grease in the pan. Stir the all purpose flour into the bacon grease. Stir constantly and cook for 1 minute. Slowly stir in the whole milk. Keep stirring and cook until the sauce thickens. Remove the pan from the heat and stir in the cheddar cheese. Add the cooked spinach and stir to combine.

Preheat the oven to 350°. Spray a 2 quart casserole dish with non stick cooking spray. Pour the spinach into the casserole dish. Sprinkle the spinach with the bread crumbs and bacon. Bake for 15-20 minutes or until the casserole is hot and the bread crumbs are brown.

Turnip Greens with Bacon

A New Year's Day must have!

Makes 6 servings

3 slices bacon, chopped
1/4 cup sliced green onions
4 garlic cloves, minced
2 cups water
2 cups peeled and chopped turnips
8 oz. smoked ham hock
1 tbs. granulated sugar
1/4 tsp. salt
1/8 tsp. ground red pepper
20 cups turnips and mustard greens
Pepper Sauce Vinegar, optional

In a large sauce pan over medium heat, cook the bacon until crisp. Remove the bacon but reserve the bacon drippings. Refrigerate the bacon and set aside for now.

In a large stock pot over medium heat, add the green onions, garlic and bacon drippings. Stir constantly and cook for 5 minutes. Slowly add the water and bring the water to a boil. Add the turnips, ham hock, granulated sugar, salt and red pepper. Place a lid on the pot and reduce the heat to low. Simmer for 45 minutes.

While the turnips are cooking, wash the greens. Fresh greens can be very dirty and dirt will hide in the leaves. Remove the stems if desired. Tear the greens into large pieces. Add the greens to the pot. Place the lid back on the pot and simmer for 20 minutes. The greens should be tender when done. Cook for a longer time if you like softer greens.

Remove the ham hock from the pot. Remove any meat from the hock and place the meat back into the pot. Add the bacon and cook until the bacon is heated. Serve with cornbread or hot biscuits for soaking up the juice. A few sprinkles of Pepper Sauce Vinegar is wonderful over the greens.

Southern Cole Slaw

Makes 8 servings

8 cups shredded cabbage
3 small carrots, grated
1 cup mayonnaise
1/4 cup whole milk
1/3 cup finely minced onion
1/2 green bell pepper, finely chopped
1 tbs. granulated sugar
1 tbs. white vinegar
Salt and black pepper to taste

In a large bowl, combine all of the ingredients except the salt and black pepper. Once the ingredients are thoroughly mixed, taste and season with salt and black pepper if desired.

English Pea Slaw

Makes 8 servings

15 oz. can English peas, drained
8 cups shredded cabbage
1 1/2 cups mayonnaise
1 tbs. granulated sugar
1/2 tsp. salt
1/2 cup grated carrot

In a large bowl, add the english peas, cabbage, mayonnaise, granulated sugar, salt and carrot. Toss to combine the ingredients. Chill for 2 hours before serving.

Tangerine Rice

Makes 4 servings

Serve with chicken, duck or turkey.

1 cup uncooked long grain rice
3 cups water
4 tbs. unsalted butter
1 seedless tangerine
1 cup chopped onion
1/3 cup frozen tangerine juice concentrate, thawed
5 oz. can sliced water chestnuts, drained
1 tsp. granulated sugar
1/2 tsp. salt

In a sauce pan over medium heat, add the water. Bring the water to a boil. Stir in the rice and place a lid on the sauce pan. Reduce the heat to low and simmer the rice about 20 minutes or until the rice is tender. Remove the pan from the heat and stir in 2 tablespoons butter. Let the rice sit in the pan while you prepare the rest of the recipe. Keep the rice warm.

Peel and section the tangerine over a bowl to catch any juice. Cut each tangerine section in half. In a skillet over medium heat, add 2 tablespoons butter and the onion. Saute the onion for 4 minutes. Reduce the heat to low. Stir in the tangerine sections and any juice, tangerine juice concentrate, water chestnuts, granulated sugar and salt. Stir constantly and bring the sauce to a boil. Remove the pan from the heat and pour the mixture over the rice. Stir lightly to combine the ingredients.

Chili Bean Salad

Makes 10 servings

2 tsp. chili powder
1/4 cup olive oil
2 tbs. vinegar
2 tsp. granulated sugar
1/4 tsp. salt
4 cups kidney beans, cooked
1 cup green bell pepper, diced
1 cup onion, diced
1 cup black olives, sliced
2 tbs. ketchup
1 tbs. mayonnaise
8 cups iceberg lettuce, torn into bite size pieces
4 oz. American cheese, sliced
2 cups salsa, optional

In a sauce pan over low heat, add the chili powder and olive oil. Stir to combine the ingredients. Simmer for 2 minutes. Do not let the olive oil boil. Add the vinegar, granulated sugar and salt. Cook for 1 minute. Remove the pan from the heat.

In a large bowl, add the olive oil mixture and the kidney beans. Toss to coat the beans in the dressing. Let the beans sit at room temperature for 30 minutes to season. Add the green bell pepper, onion, black olives, ketchup and mayonnaise. Stir to combine the ingredients.

When ready to serve, place the iceberg lettuce in a large bowl. Spoon the bean mixture over the lettuce. Place the cheese slices over the lettuce and serve. Serve with the salsa for additional dressing if desired.

Garden Row Salad

Makes 12 servings

6 carrots, finely chopped
2 cucumbers, peeled and finely chopped
8 stalks celery, finely chopped
2 pts. cherry tomatoes, halved
2 cups sharp cheddar cheese, cubed
3 cups garlic croutons
4 hard boiled eggs, sliced
12 slices bacon, cooked and crumbled
1 1/3 cups vegetable oil
1 cup ketchup
1/2 cup granulated sugar
6 tbs. fresh lemon juice
4 tbs. Worcestershire sauce
4 tbs. vinegar
4 tbs. water
2 tbs. grated onion
1 tsp. salt
1 tsp. paprika

In a jar with a lid, add the vegetable oil, ketchup, granulated sugar, lemon juice, Worcestershire sauce, vinegar, water, grated onion, salt and paprika. Place the lid on the jar and shake until the dressing is well combined. Chill for 3 hours before using.

In a large salad bowl, add the carrots, cucumbers, celery, tomatoes, bacon and cheese. Pour 1/2 the dressing over the salad. Toss to combine the salad. Place the croutons and egg slices over the top of the salad.

Place the remaining dressing on the table and allow each person to add additional dressing if needed.

Potato Vegetable Salad

Makes 6 servings

6 cups romaine lettuce, torn into bite size pieces
1/4 cup green onions, chopped
2 cups potatoes, cooked, cooled and sliced
2 cups cherry tomatoes, halved
1/4 cup fresh parsley, minced
1 cup radishes, thinly sliced
1/2 cup Feta cheese, crumbled
1 cup black olives
1/4 cup olive oil
2 tbs. fresh lemon juice
1/2 tsp. dried oregano, crumbled
1/2 tsp. salt
1/8 tsp. black pepper

Place the lettuce in a large bowl. Place the green onions, potatoes, tomatoes, fresh parsley, radishes and olives over the lettuce.

In a jar with a lid, add the olive oil, lemon juice, oregano, salt and black pepper. Place the lid on the jar and shake until well combined. Pour the dressing over the salad and toss to coat. Sprinkle the Feta cheese over the top of the salad.

Artichoke Salad

Makes 10 servings

1 cup olive oil
2/3 cup vinegar
4 tbs. water
8 onion slices
2 tbs. granulated sugar
2 garlic cloves, minced
1 tsp. salt
1/2 tsp. celery seed
1/8 tsp. black pepper
1 lb. artichoke hearts, cooked and chilled
8 cups Bibb lettuce, torn into bite size pieces
16 cherry tomatoes, halved

In a shallow bowl, add the olive oil, vinegar, water, onion slices, granulated sugar, garlic, salt, celery seed and black pepper. Stir until well combined.

Add the artichoke hearts and toss to coat the artichokes. Chill for 3-4 hours. When ready to serve, place the lettuce in a large salad bowl. Place the cherry tomatoes on top of the lettuce. Spoon the artichokes and dressing over the salad.

Stardust Salad

Makes 12 servings

4 serving size lemon jello
4 serving size orange jello
2 cups boiling water
1 1/2 cups cold water
15 oz. can crushed pineapple
1 1/2 cups miniature marshmallows
2 bananas, sliced
1 cup granulated sugar
2 tbs. all purpose flour
1 cup pineapple juice, drained from the crushed pineapple
1 egg, beaten
8 oz. Cool Whip
3 oz. pkg. cream cheese, softened

Drain the pineapple reserving the juice. In a mixing bowl, add the boiling water, lemon jello and orange jello. Stir until the jello is dissolved. Add the cold water, bananas, crushed pineapple and the marshmallows. Spoon the jello mixture into a 9 x 13 serving dish. Refrigerate the jello until firm.

You need one cup of pineapple juice. If the pineapple did not drain at least one cup of juice, then add water to make one cup. Discard if you have additional pineapple juice.

In a sauce pan over low heat, add the pineapple juice, granulated sugar, all purpose flour and beaten egg. Cook until the sauce thickens or about 5-6 minutes. Remove the sauce from the heat and refrigerate until cold. When the sauce is cold, spoon the sauce over the jello in the pan.

In a mixing bowl with a whisk, beat together the Cool Whip and the cream cheese. Spread the Cool Whip mixture over the top of the sauce. Refrigerate until serving time.

Summer Fruit Bowl

Makes 6 servings

3 bananas
4 oranges
1 cup strawberries
1 cup seedless green grapes
1/2 cup sour cream
1 tbs. honey
1 tbs. orange juice

Peel the bananas and cut into slices. Peel the oranges and cut into bite size pieces. Cut the strawberries into slices. Cut the grapes into halves. Place the fruit in a large bowl.

In a small bowl, add the sour cream, honey and orange juice. Stir to combine. Add the dressing to the fruits in the bowl. Toss to coat. Refrigerate at least 2 hours before serving.

Minted Melon Balls

These are great to serve for brunch, lunch or any summer barbecue.

Makes 4 cups

1 cup granulated sugar
1/3 cup water
1/2 cup mint leaves
4 cups watermelon balls

In a sauce pan over low heat, add the granulated sugar and water. Stir constantly and bring the syrup to a boil. Remove the pan from the heat and pour in a blender. Add the mint leaves and blend until well combined.

In a serving bowl, add the watermelon balls. Pour the mint syrup over the watermelon. Gently toss to combine the ingredients. Chill at least 3 hours before serving.

Grilled Cantaloupe Wedges

Makes 6 servings

1/4 cup vegetable oil
3 tbs. vinegar
1 tbs. minced onion
2 tsp. minced fresh thyme
Pinch of black pepper
1 large cantaloupe, peeled and cut into 12 wedges

In a small bowl, add the vegetable oil, vinegar, onion, black pepper and thyme. Stir until combined. Place 3 cantaloupe wedges on a skewer. Thread the skewer through the ends of the cantaloupe so it holds on the skewer. Repeat until all the cantaloupe wedges are on skewers.

Brush the oil mixture over the cantaloupe wedges. Place the cantaloupe on a grill over medium coals. Grill for 2-3 minutes on each side. Brush the remaining oil mixture over the cantaloupe wedges during the cooking process. Remove the cantaloupe from the grill and serve.

Deviled Eggs

Makes 12 egg halves

6 hard boiled eggs
1 tsp. prepared yellow mustard
1/4 cup real mayonnaise
Salt and pepper to taste
Paprika or cayenne pepper, optional

Peel the hard boiled eggs and slice them in half lengthwise. Gently remove the yolks from the egg white and place them in a small bowl. Lay the egg white halves on a plate and set aside. Mash the yolks with a fork until all the yolks are mashed and there are no big lumps. Add the mustard and the mayonnaise to the egg yolks and mix thoroughly. Taste the egg yolks and season with salt and pepper if desired.

Depending on the size of your eggs and the creaminess desired, you may need to add additional mayonnaise. You can add additional seasoning flavors, bacon bits, cheddar cheese or a touch of hot sauce to the mixture if desired.

Place about a tablespoon of the egg yolk filling on each egg white half. Repeat this process until all the egg whites are filled. Sprinkle with paprika or cayenne pepper if desired.

Refrigerate until ready to serve. As with any food containing mayonnaise, keep the food cool and follow food safety rules. They will keep about 3 days in the refrigerator.

Purple Hull Peas

Makes 6 servings

3 1/2 cups fresh purple hull peas
1/4 lb. Salt pork, rinsed
1 tsp. salt
2 1/2 quarts water

Wash the peas and discard any bad peas. Over medium heat, place a dutch oven or large pot on the stove top. Add the water, salt and salt pork. You can cube the salt pork or leave the chunk whole. Add the freshly washed peas and cook for 2-3 hours or until the peas are tender. Add additional water as needed to keep the peas covered and moist.

Once the peas begin to boil, reduce the heat to medium low and let them simmer on the stove until tender.

6 BREADS

I use basically one recipe for rolls for holiday dinners. I have included several bread recipes including easy ones to use for barbecues and for quick meals.

Included are several savory quick bread recipes for easy meal time bread. I like quick breads for barbecues, brunch and family dinners. When you need to put dinner on the table in a hurry, quick breads are just the ticket to round out the meal.

Sage Dinner Braid

This is an impressive bread to highlight any holiday table. It is also great for every day dinner meals, brunch or BBQ's. It never hurts the dough is super easy to make. Get the kids in on the fun!

4 cups Bisquick
1 tsp. ground sage
1/2 cup unsalted butter
1 1/3 cups whole milk
2 tsp. grated onion
1 egg, beaten

In a mixing bowl, add the Bisquick and sage. Stir until blended. Add the butter and cut the butter into the dry ingredients using a pastry blender. The mixture should look like coarse crumbles when done. You should still be able to see tiny pieces of the butter when done.

Add the milk and onion. Stir only until blended. Lightly flour your work surface. Place the dough on the work surface. Knead the dough a couple of times but do not over work the dough. Only knead until the dough holds together. Divide the dough into 18 pieces.

Roll each piece into a 12" rope. Using 3 ropes at a time, braid the bread. You should have 6 braids when done. Pinch the ends of the braids to seal the dough ends.

Place 3 braids on a cookie sheet side by side. Round the ends to form an oval shape. Place 2 braids on top of the 3 braid loaf. Center them so they are even. Place the remaining braid on top of the two braids. Brush the bread all over with the beaten egg.

Preheat the oven to 375°. Bake for 1 hour or until the bread is done and golden brown. Remove the bread from the oven and serve.

Onion Kuchen

Serve this for brunch, dinner and BBQ's.

Makes 8 servings

2 onions, sliced and separated into rings
3 tbs. unsalted butter
10 ct. can refrigerated biscuits (not Grand's)
1 egg
1 cup sour cream
1/2 tsp. salt
1 tsp. poppy seeds, optional

In a skillet over low heat, add the butter and onion rings. Do not get in a hurry to saute the onions and turn up the heat. The onions are key to the recipe and taste.

Saute the onions about 10 minutes. The onions need to be soft. Place the biscuits in an 8" layer cake pan. Press the biscuits together to completely cover the bottom of the pan. Spoon the onions over the top of the biscuits. Preheat the oven to 375°.

In a small bowl, add the egg, sour cream and salt. Whisk until well combined. Spoon the mixture over the onions. Sprinkle with poppy seeds if desired. Bake for 25-30 minutes. The biscuits should be done and the sour cream topping set. Remove the bread from the oven. Cut the bread into wedges and serve.

I like to sprinkle about 1/2 cup shredded cheddar cheese or Parmesan cheese over the onion mixture before adding the sour cream.

Cheese Loaf

This bread is very easy to make. It has a mild cheese flavor and is perfect for sandwiches, toast, stuffing and croutons. Serve with eggs, ham or make breakfast sandwiches. Use this recipe anytime you need a fresh loaf of bread.

Makes 1 loaf

3 cups self rising flour
1/4 cup granulated sugar
1 cup shredded cheddar cheese
1/2 tsp. minced dried onion
1 1/2 cups whole milk
1/4 cup vegetable oil

Preheat the oven to 350°. Spray a loaf pan with non stick cooking spray. In a mixing bowl, add the self rising flour, granulated sugar, cheddar cheese and onion. Stir until well combined.

Stir in the milk and vegetable oil. Mix only until combined and a dough forms. Press the dough into the prepared loaf pan. Bake for 45-55 minutes. The bread should be golden brown and sound hollow when tapped. Remove the bread from the oven and cool the bread for 10 minutes in the pan.

Remove the bread from the pan and cool completely before slicing.

Ribbon Cheese Loaf

This makes an easy and impressive dish. Serve the bread for brunch, holiday dinners or supper.

Makes one loaf

24 refrigerated flaky rolls or biscuits (not Grand's)
1 cup shredded sharp cheddar cheese
1 tbs. melted unsalted butter
1/2 tsp. dried parsley flakes

Separate the rolls from the can. Cut each roll into 3 pieces. Spray a loaf pan with non stick cooking spray. Place 24 pieces in the bottom of the loaf pan. Sprinkle half the cheese over the pieces. Place 24 more pieces on top of the cheese. Sprinkle the remaining cheese over the bread pieces. Place the remaining pieces in the loaf pan over the cheese. Brush the melted butter over the bread. Sprinkle the parsley over the top of the bread.

Preheat the oven to 375°. Bake for 30-40 minutes or until the bread is golden brown and the rolls are done. Remove the loaf from the oven and cool for 5 minutes in the pan. Remove the bread from the pan and serve.

You can add any number of seasonings to the bread for variety. Dried minced onion, garlic, Italian seasoning, cumin and chili powder make great seasonings for this bread. Use the seasonings based upon the meal you are serving.

For an Italian dinner use garlic and Italian seasonings, for a Mexican meal use cumin and chili powder, etc.

Herb Cheese Pull Apart Rolls

These rolls are so easy to make and they are perfect with grilled meats.

Makes 8 servings

8 oz. pkg. cream cheese, softened
1 tsp. dried parsley flakes
1 tsp. dried basil
1 tsp. minced fresh chives
1/2 tsp. dried dill
1/8 tsp. garlic powder
8 ct. can refrigerated crescent rolls
1 egg, beaten

Preheat the oven to 375°. In a mixing bowl, add the cream cheese, parsley flakes, basil, chives, dill and garlic powder. Stir until well combined.

Unroll the crescent roll dough into a rectangle. Press the perforations to seal all the seams. Spread the cream cheese mixture over the dough leaving about a 1/2" edge with no cream cheese. Starting with a long side, roll the dough up like a jelly roll. Pinch the edges together to seal. With sharp kitchen scissors, cut 1/2" slices in the dough. Do not cut the dough all the way through. Alternate sides cutting one on the right and then one on the left. Slightly separate the slices so you can see the filling.

Spray a baking sheet with non stick cooking spray. Place the roll on the baking sheet. Brush the beaten egg over the roll. Bake for 10-15 minutes or until the crescent rolls are done and golden brown. Remove the rolls from the oven and serve.

Do not worry if you mess up cutting the rolls. The pattern is only decorative, keeps the filling in tact and it helps the rolls cook evenly. They will be delicious no matter how you cut them.

Perfect Sunday Dinner Rolls

Makes 24 crescent shaped rolls

These are the only rolls my mother made for holidays and Sunday dinner.

1 pkg. regular yeast dissolved in 1/4 cup warm water
1/2 cup granulated sugar
2 eggs
1 cup warm water
1/2 cup vegetable oil
1 tsp. salt
4 cups all purpose flour
Additional flour for rolling
Melted unsalted butter for dipping rolls

In a large mixing bowl, add the dissolved yeast and the granulated sugar. Stir to mix. With an electric mixer or whisk, beat in the eggs, oil, salt and one cup of warm water. Add the all purpose flour and mix to combine. The dough will look shaggy and this dough is not kneaded.

The dough will rise very high so use a large bowl. Cover the bowl with plastic wrap and place the dough in the refrigerator overnight.

Lightly grease two baking sheets. After the dough has risen overnight, lightly flour your work surface. Divide the dough into 3 parts. Roll each part into a round 10" circle. With a pizza cutter or a sharp knife, cut the dough into 8 wedges for each 10" circle. The easiest way to do this is to cut the dough circle into fourths and then each fourth into two parts. Starting with the large end, roll toward the small end just like a crescent roll. Dip the rolls in melted butter and place on the greased cookie sheet.

My mother's instructions are to let the rolls rise in a warm place until you get home from church or about two hours. Preheat the oven to 375°. Pop them in the oven and bake for 8-10 minutes. They will be golden brown and very fluffy.

Onion Biscuits

Serve these biscuits with ham, bacon, sausage or most any meat.

Makes about 10 biscuits

3/4 cup finely chopped onion
2 tbs. unsalted butter
1/4 cup vegetable shortening
1 1/2 cups all purpose flour
1 1/2 tsp. baking powder
1/2 tsp. salt
1 tsp. celery seed
1 beaten egg
1/3 cup whole milk

In a small sauce pan over medium heat, add the onion and butter. Saute the onion for 4 minutes or until the onion is soft. Remove the pan from the heat.

In a mixing bowl, add the all purpose flour, baking powder, salt, celery seed and vegetable shortening. Using a pastry blender, cut the shortening into the dry ingredients. The dough should resemble coarse crumbs. You should still be able to see tiny pieces of shortening when done. Stir in the onion and butter.

Add the egg and milk. Mix only until a dough forms and leaves the side of the bowl. Preheat the oven to 450°. Lightly flour your work surface. Place the dough on the work surface. Knead the dough a couple of times until the dough holds together. Pat the dough to a 1/2" thickness. Using a 2" biscuit cutter, cut out the biscuits. Place the biscuits on an ungreased baking pan. Roll the scraps and cut out any remaining biscuits.

Bake for 12-15 minutes or until the biscuits are done and golden brown. Serve the biscuits hot.

Super Fast Garlic Bread Sticks

This recipe is a huge time saver. I serve it with hearty dips as an appetizer or with dinner meals.

Makes 24 sticks

6 slices bread (use your favorite kind)
6 tbs. unsalted butter, softened
2 garlic cloves, crushed
1/4 cup grated Parmesan cheese

Trim the crust from the bread if desired. I trim the crust if serving for a party but leave them on just for the family. In a small bowl, add the butter and garlic. Stir until well combined. Spread the butter over both sides of the bread. Sprinkle the Parmesan cheese over the bread.

Preheat the oven to 300°. Cut each bread slice into 4 strips. Place the strips on a baking sheet. Bake for 18-20 minutes. Turn the bread sticks over halfway through the baking time. Both sides of the bread sticks should be golden brown when ready. Remove the bread sticks from the oven and serve.

Store leftover cooled bread sticks in a plastic bag.

Salty No Yeast Bread Sticks

Makes 18 bread sticks

1 1/2 cups all purpose flour
2 tsp. baking powder
1/2 tsp. salt
1/2 cup plain yellow or white cornmeal
3 tbs. vegetable shortening
1/2 cup whole milk
1 egg
Coarse salt
Water

Preheat the oven to 450°. In a mixing bowl, add the all purpose flour, baking powder, salt, cornmeal and vegetable shortening. Using a pastry blender, cut the shortening into the dry ingredients. The mixture should resemble coarse crumbs. You should still be able to see tiny pieces of the shortening when ready.

Stir in the milk and egg. Stir only until a dough forms and the dough leaves the side of the bowl. Turn the dough onto a lightly floured work surface. Knead the dough a few times until the dough smooths out.

Divide the dough into 18 pieces. Roll each dough piece in your hands to a pencil like shape about 6" long. Spray a baking sheet with non stick cooking spray. Place the bread sticks on the baking sheet. Brush the bread sticks with water. Sprinkle the coarse salt over the bread sticks.

Bake for 15-18 minutes. The bread sticks should be crispy and browned.

You can use any seasoning you like instead of the salt.

7 DESSERTS: PIES, CAKES, COOKIES & CANDIES

Perfect desserts for perfect meals. Make any of the desserts in this cookbook and your guest will fondly remember them.

Several cakes and pies are always served for the holidays. To this day, they are still my favorite part of holiday meals. I always have to eat a thin slice of every dessert.

I have included many homemade candy recipes. My mother made candy every Christmas and Easter. Fudge bunnies and fudge cut out with cookie cutters were delicious.

Use cookie cutters and make any number of different designs for your fudge. Use the pan stated in the recipe or spread the fudge in a large pan for thinner cut outs. Press the cookie cutters into the hard and cooled fudge. Remove the fudge cut outs with an offset spatula. Decorate the fudge if desired.

You can also spray your cookie cutters with non stick cooking spray. Place the cookie cutters on a baking sheet. Fill the cookie cutters with the hot fudge. Cool completely and remove the cookie cutters. Decorate the fudge if desired.

It would not be the holidays without decorated cookies. I have included my favorite recipes for sugar cookies.

Pie Crust

This recipe is for one 9" pie crust. Double the ingredients if you need a double crust pie. This is the only recipe my mother used and it is wonderfully flaky. The unbaked pie crust freezes well.

1 1/4 cups all purpose flour
1/4 cup unsalted butter
1/4 cup lard or vegetable shortening
1/4 tsp. salt
Ice water

In a bowl, add the all purpose flour and the salt. Chop the butter into small pieces and add to the flour. Add the lard or vegetable shortening. With a pastry blender or your fingers, work the butter and lard into the all purpose flour.

The butter and lard pieces should be very small and no larger than a small pea. Add just enough ice water to bring the flour mixture into a ball. You don't want to add too much ice water. I usually add 1 tablespoon in the beginning and then 1/2 tablespoon at a time until it reaches the dough consistency I need. This will be a soft dough unless the butter and lard are still very cold.

Turn the dough onto a lightly floured board and knead a couple of times. You don't want to handle it too much but just enough to form a good dough.

Wrap plastic wrap around the pie dough and refrigerate for one hour before using. The dough needs to be cold when you roll it out. It is imperative the pie crust be cold before placing the crust in the oven.

The butter and lard when cold will "fluff up" and create the flakiness we love in a beautiful pie crust.

If you need a baked pie crust unfilled, place the pie crust in a 9" pie pan and bake about 12-15 minutes at 350°. I prick the bottom of my pie crust several times with a fork. This ensures the pie crust will not puff up when baking.

Grandma's Chocolate Pie

Makes a 9" pie

9" baked prepared pie crust
1 1/2 cups granulated sugar
2 tbs. cornstarch
2 tbs. unsweetened baking cocoa
1 1/2 cups whole milk
2 tbs. unsalted butter
Dash of salt
2 egg yolks, separated
1 tbs. vanilla extract

In a sauce pan over medium heat, add the granulated sugar, cornstarch, baking cocoa, milk, egg yolks and salt. Stir constantly and cook for 7-8 minutes or until thickened. Once the filling thickens to pudding consistency, remove the pan from the heat.

Stir in the butter and vanilla extract. Let the filling cool while you prepare the meringue.

Preheat the oven to 425°. In a clean mixing bowl with a mixer set on medium speed, add the egg whites. Beat for several minutes or until stiff peaks form.

Spoon the filling into the prepared pie crust. Spread the meringue over the filling. Make certain the meringue goes all the way to the edge of the pie crust. If the meringue does not meet the edge of the pie crust, it will shrink and weep. This will make for a soggy meringue.

Bake for 5-6 minutes or until the meringue browns. Meringue will brown fast so watch it closely.

Pecan Pie

Makes a 9" pie

9" unbaked pie crust, prepared
1 cup light corn syrup
1 cup dark brown sugar
3 eggs, beaten
1/3 cup unsalted butter, melted
1/2 tsp. salt
1 tsp. vanilla extract
1 cup pecan halves

Preheat the oven to 350°. In a large mixing bowl, add the corn syrup, brown sugar, eggs, butter, salt and vanilla extract. Using a whisk, beat until well combined. Stir in the pecans.

Pour the filling into the pie crust. Bake for 45-50 minutes or until the center of the pie is set. Remove the pie from the oven and serve warm or cold.

Note: If the pie crust edges are browning too fast, cover the edges with aluminum foil.

Chocolate Pecan Pie

Makes a 9" deep dish pie

1 1/2 cups light corn syrup
1/4 cup granulated sugar
1/4 cup unsalted butter
9" prepared pie crust, unbaked
1 cup pecans
1 cup semi sweet chocolate chips
3 eggs
1 tsp. vanilla extract

Preheat the oven to 375°. In a large sauce pan over medium heat, add the corn syrup, granulated sugar and butter. Stir constantly and bring the mixture to a boil. Boil for 2 minutes. Remove the pan from the heat and cool to lukewarm.

Place the pecans and the chocolate chips in the prepared pie crust. In a small bowl, add the eggs and the vanilla extract. Beat vigorously with a whisk for 3 minutes. Pour the eggs into the cooled corn syrup mixture. Beat for 3 minutes or until well combined. Pour this batter over the pecans and chocolate chips in the pie crust.

Bake for 40-45 minutes or until the center of the pie is firm. Serve warm or cold.

Top each serving with Cool Whip if desired.

Chocolate Chess Pie

Makes a 8" pie

1/2 cup melted unsalted butter
2 tbs. unsweetened baking cocoa powder
2 1/2 cups granulated sugar
2 eggs
2/3 cup evaporated milk
1 1/2 tsp. vanilla extract
Unbaked 8" pie crust

Preheat the oven to 350°. In a mixing bowl, add the melted butter, granulated sugar and the cocoa. With an electric mixer on medium speed, beat the butter mixture about 1 minute. Add the eggs, evaporated milk and vanilla extract.

Continue beating until well combined or about 2 minutes. Pour the pie batter into the prepared pie crust and bake for 30-40 minutes or until the pie is set. Do not over bake this pie as it will continue cooking for a few minutes when removed from the oven. The pie should be set but still jiggle slightly when ready.

Southern Chess Pie

Makes a 9" pie

Unbaked 9" pie crust
1/2 cup melted unsalted butter
3 eggs
1 tsp. vanilla extract
1/4 cup whole milk
1 1/2 cups granulated sugar
Pinch of salt

Preheat the oven to 350°. In a mixing bowl, add the melted butter and the granulated sugar. With an electric mixer on medium speed, beat for 2 minutes. Add the eggs, salt, vanilla extract and whole milk. Beat for 2 minutes.

Pour the pie batter into the prepared pie pan. Bake for 30-35 minutes or until the top is golden brown and the center is set. The pie will jiggle slightly when done. Do not over bake this pie as it will cook for a few minutes after removing from the oven.

Lemon Chess Pie

Makes a 9" pie

4 eggs
2 cups granulated sugar
1/2 cup lemon juice
1/2 cup melted unsalted butter
1 tsp. all purpose flour
1/8 tsp. salt
Unbaked 9" pie crust

Add the eggs to a large mixing bowl. Beat with an electric mixer on high speed until the eggs are blended and lemon colored. This will take about 3-4 minutes. Gradually add the granulated sugar and continue to beat until the sugar is well combined with the eggs.

Turn the mixer to low speed and add the lemon juice, melted butter, all purpose flour and the salt. Pour the batter into the prepared unbaked pie crust. Bake the pie for 35-40 minutes or until the the pie is set and the top golden brown. The center of the pie should be set but still jiggle slightly when done.

Do not over bake this pie as it will continue to cook when removed from the oven. Cool completely before serving.

Pineapple Chess Pie

Makes two 9" pies

16 oz. can crushed pineapple, drained
4 eggs
4 cups granulated sugar
1 tsp. vanilla extract
1 cup unsalted butter, melted
4 tbs. all purpose flour
2 unbaked 9" pie crust

Preheat the oven to 300°. In a large mixing bowl, add the drained pineapple, eggs, granulated sugar, vanilla extract, melted butter and the all purpose flour. With a whisk, mix together until the ingredients are well incorporated.

Pour half the batter into each pie shell. Bake for 1 hour or until the pie is set. The center of the pie will jiggle slightly when done. Do not over bake this pie as it will continue to firm up and cook while cooling.

Apple Crumb Pie

Makes a 9" pie

6 cups chopped apples, peeled & cored
2 tbs. unsalted butter, melted
2 tbs. sour cream
4 tsp. lemon juice
1 cup granulated sugar
1/2 cup plus 1 tbs. all purpose flour
1/2 tsp. ground cinnamon
1/2 tsp. ground nutmeg
9" pie crust, unbaked
1/4 cup unsalted butter, chilled

Place the pie crust in a 9" pie pan if you have not already prepared the crust. Preheat the oven to 375°. In a mixing bowl, add the apples, melted butter, sour cream, lemon juice, 1/2 cup granulated sugar, 1 tablespoon all purpose flour, cinnamon and nutmeg. Toss to coat the apples with the ingredients. Spoon the apples into the prepared pie crust.

In a small bowl, add 1/2 cup granulated sugar, 1/4 cup chilled butter and 1/2 cup all purpose flour. Using your fingers, work the butter into the dry ingredients until you have coarse crumbs. Sprinkle the crumbs over the apples. Bake for 45-50 minutes or until the apples are tender and the crumbs golden brown.

Remove the pie from the oven and cool the pie for 15 minutes before serving.
Serve the pie warm or cold.

Brown Sugar Peach Pie

Makes a 9" pie

Pie dough for double crust pie
3/4 cup light brown sugar
1/3 cup all purpose flour
3 tbs. light corn syrup
1 tbs. lemon juice
1/3 cup unsalted butter, softened
6 fresh peaches, sliced and peeled

Preheat the oven to 400°. Roll out half of the pie dough to a 11" circle. Place the pie crust in a 9" pie pan. Trim the excess dough from the edges if desired. In a mixing bowl, add the brown sugar, all purpose flour, corn syrup, lemon juice and butter. Stir until well combined.

Place the peaches, pit side down, in the pie crust. Pour the brown sugar mixture over the peaches. Roll out the remaining pie dough to form a lattice crust or double crust pie.

To make a double crust pie, roll out the remaining pie dough to a 12" circle. Place the dough over the pie filling. Trim and flute the edges as desired. Cut six 1" slits in the top of the pie crust. Bake for 30-40 minutes or until the peaches are tender and the filling set. Remove the pie from the oven and cool completely before serving.

You can substitute 3 1/2 cups well drained canned peach slices for the fresh peaches if desired.

Cherry Pie

Makes a 9" pie

Pie dough for double crust pie
1 1/2 cups granulated sugar
4 tbs. cornstarch
3/4 cup cherry juice
3 cups canned pitted red cherries
1 tbs. unsalted butter
1/4 tsp. red food coloring, optional

Roll out one half of the pie dough to a 11" circle. Place the dough in a 9" pie pan. Trim the edges if desired. Preheat the oven to 400°.

In a sauce pan over medium low heat, add 3/4 cup granulated sugar, cornstarch and the cherry juice. Stir until well combined. Stir constantly and cook until the mixture begins to boil. Cook for 1 minute after the mixture boils. Add the remaining 3/4 cup granulated sugar, cherries, butter and food coloring. Stir until well combined and the cherries are hot.

Spoon the cherry filling into the prepared pie crust. Roll out the remaining pie dough to a 11" circle. Place the dough over the pie filling. Trim and flute the edges as desired. Cut six 1" slits in the top of the pie crust. Place the pie on a baking sheet to catch any drips. Bake for 45-55 minutes or until the cherries are tender and the crust golden brown. Remove the pie from the oven and let the pie cool for 30 minutes before serving.

If the pie crust is browning too fast, cover the pie loosely with aluminum foil to prevent the crust from burning.

Pumpkin Pie

Makes one 9" pie

1 1/4 cups cooked or canned pumpkin, mashed
3/4 cup granulated sugar
1 tsp. ground cinnamon
1 tsp. all purpose flour
1 cup evaporated milk
1/2 tsp. vanilla extract
1/2 tsp. salt
1/4 tsp. ground ginger
2 eggs, beaten
2 tbs. water
9" unbaked prepared pie crust

Preheat the oven to 400°. In a mixing bowl, add the pumpkin, granulated sugar, salt, ginger, cinnamon and the all purpose flour. Use a whisk to combine the ingredients.

Add the evaporated milk, vanilla extract, eggs and water. Continue to whisk until well combined. This will take a few minutes. Pour the filling into the prepared pie crust. Bake for 45-50 minutes or until a knife inserted in the center of the pie comes out clean.

Serve warm or cold. It is delicious with a dollop of Cool Whip.

Pumpkin Praline Pie

Makes a 9" deep dish pie

1 cup plus 1 tbs. all purpose flour
1 tsp. salt
1/3 cup plus 1 tbs. vegetable shortening
2-3 tbs. ice cold water
1 1/2 cups light brown sugar
1/2 cup chopped pecans
3 tbs. unsalted butter, softened
1 cup canned pumpkin
1/2 tsp. ground cinnamon
1 cup evaporated milk
2 eggs
1/4 tsp. ground cloves
1/2 tsp. ground ginger

To make the pie crust, add 1 cup all purpose flour, 1/2 teaspoon salt and the vegetable shortening to a mixing bowl. Using a pastry cutter or your fingers, work the vegetable shortening into the flour and salt. You should have coarse crumbs when the dough is ready for the liquid. Add 2 tablespoons ice cold water to the dough and mix to combine. If the dough feels dry, add 1/2 to 1 tablespoon additional cold water. The dough should form into a ball. Cover the dough with plastic wrap. Place the dough to rest in the refrigerator for 30 minutes.

Once the dough has rested, roll the dough out to about 1/4" thickness on a lightly floured surface. Roll the dough out large enough to cover the deep dish pie pan. Place the crust in the pie pan and flute the edges if desired. Cut off any crust hanging over the edge of the pie plate.

Preheat the oven to 375°. In the food processor, add the pecans, 1/2 cup brown sugar and softened butter. Process until the mixture looks line a fine paste. Press the crumb mixture into the bottom of the pie crust. Press it down firmly into the pie crust to ensure it will not rise during baking. Do not damage the pie crust. If you see that you have made a hole in the pie crust, pinch the crust together to close the hole in the pie crust.

In a large mixing bowl with a mixer on medium speed, add the eggs. Beat the eggs for 2 minutes. Turn the mixer to low or beat the rest of the pie with a whisk.

Add 3/4 cup brown sugar, pumpkin, 1 tablespoon all purpose flour, cinnamon, evaporated milk, cloves, ginger and 1/2 teaspoon salt. Stir until well combined. Pour the filling into the pie crust. Bake for 45-50 minutes checking the pie frequently to make sure you do not over cook the pie.

The pie will be done when the center is firm but still jiggly when you move the pie.

Sweet Potato Pie

The ultimate southern holiday pie!

Makes an 8" pie

Pie crust for 8" single crust pie, prepared
1 1/2 cups cooked sweet potatoes, mashed
1/2 cup light brown sugar
1/2 tsp. salt
1/2 tsp. ground cinnamon
3/4 cup evaporated milk
2 eggs, beaten
1 tbs. unsalted butter, melted

Preheat the oven to 400°. In a mixing bowl, add the sweet potatoes, brown sugar, salt, butter, cinnamon, milk and eggs. Whisk together until smooth and the ingredients are well combined. Spoon the filling into the prepared pie crust.

Bake for 30-40 minutes or until a knife tip inserted off center of the pie comes out clean.

Do not over cook this pie. The filling will continue to firm up as it cools. A great sweet potato pie is moist and fluffy but set. If you insert a knife halfway between the crust and the center, it should come out clean when the pie is done.

Cajun Sweet Potato Pie

Makes a 9" pie

Unbaked 9' pie crust, prepared
1 cup light brown sugar
1 tsp. ground cinnamon
1/2 tsp. ground ginger
1/2 tsp. ground nutmeg
1/2 tsp. salt
1/8 tsp. ground cloves
2 cups mashed cooked sweet potatoes
3 eggs, beaten
1 1/2 cups hot whole milk
1/2 cup pecan halves

Preheat the oven to 375°. In a mixing bowl, add the brown sugar, cinnamon, ginger, nutmeg, salt, cloves, sweet potatoes and eggs. Stir until well combined. Add the hot milk and whisk until the pie filling is smooth. Pour the filling into the pie shell.

Bake for 25 minutes. Remove the pie from the oven and place the pecan halves over the top of the pie. Bake for 30 minutes or until the center of the pie is firm.

Sweet potato pie is easy to over bake. When the center of the filling is set, the pie is ready.

Walnut Cranberry Pie

Makes a 9" pie

3 1/2 cups fresh cranberries
1/2 cup raisins
3/4 cup chopped walnuts
1 1/2 cups granulated sugar
3 tbs. all purpose flour
1/4 cup light corn syrup
1 tsp. grated orange zest
1/4 tsp. salt
1 tbs. unsalted butter, softened
9" unbaked pie crust

Preheat the oven to 375°. In a food processor, add the cranberries and raisins. Blend until the cranberries are ground or finely chopped. Spoon the cranberries and raisins into a bowl.

Stir in the walnuts, granulated sugar, all purpose flour, corn syrup, orange zest, salt and butter. Stir until well combined. Spoon the filling into the pie crust. Bake for 40-45 minutes. The pie should be set in the center when done. Remove the pie from the oven and cool before serving.

Marshmallow Coconut Pie

Makes an 8" pie

8" baked prepared pie crust
6 tbs. granulated sugar
2 egg yolks
1/2 cup all purpose flour
1 1/2 cups whole milk
1/4 cup unsalted butter
1 cup miniature marshmallows
1 1/2 cups sweetened flaked coconut
1 1/2 cups Cool Whip

In a sauce pan over medium heat, add the granulated sugar, egg yolks, all purpose flour, milk and butter. Stir constantly and cook for 7-8 minutes or until the pie filling is combined and thickened.

Remove the pan from the heat and stir in the marshmallows and 1 cup coconut. Stir until the marshmallows melt. Pour the filling into the baked and cooled crust.

Refrigerate the pie until the filling is cool. Spread the Cool Whip over the filling. Sprinkle the remaining 1/2 cup coconut over the Cool Whip. Refrigerate for 1 hour before serving.

Coconut Cream Pie

Makes a 9" pie

1 baked and cooled 9" pie crust
1/2 cup all purpose flour
1 cup granulated sugar
1 cup whole milk
3 eggs, separated
1/2 cup unsalted butter
1 tsp. vanilla extract
2 cups sweetened, flaked coconut
6 tbs. granulated sugar

In a sauce pan over medium heat, add the all purpose flour, granulated sugar and the whole milk. Stir with a whisk until well combined. Add the egg yolks and continue to stir until the filling begins to thicken. Add the butter and cook until the filling becomes thick. Remove the pan from the heat and stir in the vanilla extract and 1 3/4 cups flaked coconut. Spoon the filling into the prepared pie crust.

Preheat the oven to 400°. In a large bowl, add 3 egg whites and the 6 tablespoons granulated sugar. Beat with a mixer on high speed until stiff peaks form. Spread the egg whites over the pie filling. Sprinkle the remaining 1/4 cup flaked coconut over the egg whites. Bake for 10-20 minutes or until the meringue is golden brown.

Praline Pie

Makes 6 servings

9" pie crust, unbaked
1/3 cup unsalted butter
1/2 cup light brown sugar
1/3 cup chopped pecans
4 serving size pkg. cook & serve vanilla pudding mix
2 cups milk
8 oz. container Cool Whip, thawed

Preheat the oven to 350°. Bake the pie crust for 5 minutes. Remove the pie crust from the oven. In a sauce pan over low heat, add the butter, brown sugar and chopped pecans. Stir constantly and cook only until the butter melts and the ingredients are well combined. Pour the mixture into the bottom of the pie crust.

Bake for 5 minutes or until the crust is done and golden brown. Let the pie crust cool completely before proceeding to the next step.

In a sauce pan over low heat, add the pudding mix and milk. Stir until the pudding thickens. Remove the pan from the heat as soon as the pudding is thick and bubbly. Cool the pudding before using.

When the pudding is cool, reserve 1 cup pudding and mix in a bowl with the Cool Whip. Pour the remaining pudding from the pan into the pie shell. Spoon the Cool Whip mixture over the top of the pudding.

Refrigerate for 3 hours before serving.

Blackberry Apple Pie

Serve this pie at Thanksgiving or barbecues.

Makes a 9" pie

Pie dough for double crust pie
3 cups fresh blackberries or frozen blackberries, thawed
1 cup peeled and thinly sliced apples
1 cup granulated sugar
3 tbs. quick cooking tapioca
1/2 tsp. ground cinnamon
2 tbs. unsalted butter

Preheat the oven to 350°. Roll out one portion of the pie crust to a 11" circle on a lightly floured surface. Place the dough in a 9" pie pan. Trim and flute the edges if desired.

Place the blackberries and apples in the pie crust. In a small bowl, add the granulated sugar, tapioca and cinnamon. Stir until well combined. Sprinkle the mixture over the fruit. Cut the butter into small pieces. Place the butter pieces over the fruit.

Roll out the remaining pie crust on a lightly floured surface. Place the pie crust over the fruit. Seal the edges to the pan. Trim and flute the edges if desired. Cut six 1" slits in the top of the pie crust. Bake for 50-60 minutes. The pie should be golden brown and the filling bubbly. Remove the pie from the oven. Cool the pie at least one hour before serving.

Coconut Cake

Makes three 9" layers

In my house, you have to make at least one coconut cake for Christmas. This is the recipe I use every time.

3/4 cup softened unsalted butter
1 1/2 cups granulated sugar
2 tsp. vanilla extract
2 3/4 cups cake flour
4 tsp. baking powder
3/4 tsp. salt
1 cup whole milk
4 eggs whites at room temperature
Coconut Frosting recipe below

Preheat the oven to 350°. Grease and flour three 9" cake pans. In a large mixing bowl, beat the egg whites until stiff peaks form. In a separate bowl, add the butter and granulated sugar. Beat with a mixer on medium speed about 4 minutes. The mixture should be light and fluffy. Add the vanilla extract and mix until combined.

Combine the cake flour, baking powder and salt in a separate bowl. Reduce the mixer speed to low and alternate adding the flour mixture and the milk. Mix only until blended.

Carefully fold in the stiffly beaten egg whites. Divide the cake batter evenly between the pans and bake for 13-17 minutes or until a toothpick inserted in the center of the cakes test clean. Cool the cake in the pan for 10 minutes. Remove the cakes from the pans and cool completely before frosting.

Coconut Frosting: In a heavy saucepan, combine 2 cups granulated sugar, 3 egg whites at room temperature and 1/2 cup water. With a mixer on low speed, beat for 1 minute. Place the sauce pan over low heat and continue beating with the mixer. Place a candy thermometer on the the sauce pan and continue beating until the frosting reaches 160°. This takes about 8-10 minutes.

Pour the saucepan ingredients into a large bowl and add 1 teaspoon vanilla extract. Continue beating the frosting until you have stiff peaks. Frost the cake and sprinkle 1/2 cup sweetened coconut on each layer after you have applied the frosting. Place 1/2 cup of sweetened coconut on the top and the sides. Store the cake in the refrigerator.

Southern Red Velvet Cake

Makes three 9" layers

2 1/2 cups self rising flour
1 cup whole milk
1 1/2 cups granulated sugar
1 1/2 cups vegetable oil
3 eggs
1 oz. red food coloring
1 tsp. vanilla extract
1 tsp. white vinegar
1 tsp. baking soda
1 tsp. unsweetened cocoa powder
Red Velvet Icing recipe in this book

Preheat the oven to 350°. Sift the self rising flour, baking soda and unsweetened cocoa together in a bowl.

In a separate bowl, add the vegetable oil and granulated sugar. Beat on medium speed with a mixer until well blended. Add the eggs, one at a time, while continuing to mix. Each egg should be mixed thoroughly into the batter before you add the next egg.

Reduce the speed on the mixer to low. Add half of the flour mixture, then half of the milk while continuing to beat with the mixer. Repeat until the flour and milk are gone. Add in the white vinegar, vanilla extract and red food coloring. Mix to combine the liquids. The cake should have a nice red color.

Grease your cake pans or spray them with non stick cooking spray. Divide the batter evenly between the three cake pans. Bake for 20-30 minutes or until the cakes test done. A toothpick inserted in the center should come out clean. Cool the layers completely in the pan before frosting. While the cakes are cooling, make the icing.

Red Velvet Cake Icing

Cream cheese frosting is not traditional for a Red Velvet Cake in the South. This is a traditional southern Red Velvet cake icing.

1 cup whole milk
1/4 cup all purpose flour
1/8 tsp. salt
2 tsp. vanilla extract
1 cup granulated sugar
1/2 cup unsalted butter
1/2 cup Crisco shortening

In a small saucepan over medium low heat, add the whole milk, salt and all purpose flour. Stir constantly and cook until thick. Remove the pan from the heat and place the mixture in the refrigerator until cool.

When the milk mixture is cool, add it to a large mixing bowl. Add the granulated sugar, vanilla extract, butter and Crisco. Beat with a mixer on medium speed at least 6-8 minutes. The longer you beat this frosting, the smoother and fluffier it will be. Spread on your cooled Red Velvet cake.

Southern Caramel Cake

Makes three 9" layers

3 cups cake flour
3 tsp. baking powder
1/2 tsp. salt
1 cup softened unsalted butter
1 cup granulated sugar
1 cup light brown sugar
4 eggs
1 cup whole milk
1 tsp. vanilla extract
Caramel Icing below

Grease and flour three 9" cake pans. Preheat the oven to 350°. In a small bowl, sift together the cake flour, baking powder and salt. Set aside. In a large mixing bowl, add the butter, granulated sugar and brown sugar. Beat with a mixer on medium speed until light and fluffy or about 4 minutes. Add the eggs and vanilla extract. Beat for 3 minutes. While continuously mixing, alternate adding the flour mixture and the whole milk.

Only mix long enough to combine the flour and milk. Do not over beat the batter. Divide the batter evenly between the cake pans. Bake for 20-25 minutes or until the center of the cakes test done with a toothpick. Remove the cakes from the oven and cool completely before frosting.

Caramel Icing: In a heavy sauce pan, add 3/4 cup unsalted butter. Melt the butter over low heat. Gradually stir in 2 cups light brown sugar. Continuously stirring, cook over low heat until the brown sugar melts and is no longer grainy.

Remove the pan from the heat and cool completely. In a mixing bowl, add 2 1/2 cups powdered sugar, 1/2 teaspoon salt and 2 tablespoons milk. Add the cooled brown sugar mixture. Beat with a mixer until smooth and fluffy. Sometimes this icing is thinner than desired. Add additional powdered sugar to make the icing consistency you want.

Mountain Dew Cake

Makes three 8" layers

4 serving size orange jello
4 serving size coconut cream pie pudding mix
1 cup vegetable oil
1 box orange cake mix
4 eggs
1 1/4 cups Mountain Dew
20 oz. can crushed pineapple
8 oz. can crushed pineapple
5 tbs. all purpose flour
1/4 cup unsalted butter
2 cups granulated sugar
2 cups sweetened flaked coconut

Preheat the oven to 350°. Grease three 8" cake pans with non stick cooking spray. In a mixing bowl, add the orange cake mix, jello, coconut pudding mix, eggs, vegetable oil and Mountain Dew. Beat with a mixer on medium speed for 4 minutes. Pour the batter into the cake pans. Bake 15-25 minutes or until the cake test done in the center with a toothpick. Cool completely before frosting.

To make the frosting, in a sauce pan over medium heat, add both cans of pineapple with the juice, all purpose flour and granulated sugar. Stir to combine the ingredients. Bring the mixture to a simmer and cook until thick. Remove the pan from the stove and add the butter and the coconut. Spread on the cooled cake.

Carrot Cake

Makes three 9" cake pans

For Easter in my house, we have to have a carrot cake and a coconut cake. The family would kill me if both cakes were not made.

2 cups all purpose flour
1 1/2 tsp. baking soda
2 tsp. ground cinnamon
1 1/2 cups vegetable oil
2 cups shredded carrots
8 oz. can crushed pineapple, drained
2 tsp. baking powder
1 1/2 tsp. salt
2 cups granulated sugar
4 eggs
1/2 cup chopped pecans
1/2 cup unsalted butter, softened
8 oz. pkg. cream cheese, softened
1 tsp. vanilla extract
4 cups powdered sugar

Preheat the oven to 350°. Spray three 9" cake pans with non stick cooking spray.

In a large mixing bowl, add the eggs, vegetable oil and granulated sugar. Using a mixer on medium speed, beat for 4 minutes. Add the carrots, pineapple and pecans. Beat for 1 minute.

Reduce the mixer speed to low and add the all purpose flour, baking soda, cinnamon, baking powder and salt. Beat until well combined. Pour the batter evenly into the prepared cake pans. Bake for 25-30 minutes or until the cakes test done in the center with a toothpick. Remove the cakes from the oven and cool completely before frosting.

In a large mixing bowl using a mixer set on medium speed, add the softened butter and cream cheese. Beat for 4 minutes or until the butter and cream cheese are well combined. Add the vanilla extract and powdered sugar. Beat for 3 minutes. The frosting should be light, fluffy and spreadable. Spread the frosting on the cool cake layers.

Note: If the frosting is too thick, add a teaspoon or two of whole milk to thin the frosting.

German Chocolate Cake

Makes three 8" layers

4 oz. German sweet baking chocolate, chopped into small pieces
1/2 cup water
1 cup unsalted butter, softened
2 cups granulated sugar
4 eggs, separated
1 tsp. vanilla extract
2 1/2 cups cake flour
1 tsp. baking soda
1/2 tsp. salt
1 cup whole milk
Coconut Pecan Frosting recipe in this book

Line three 8" round cake pans with waxed paper. Spray the waxed paper with non stick cooking spray. This cake will stick easily, so do not skip this step.

Preheat the oven to 350°. In a small saucepan over low heat, add the German chocolate and water. Stir constantly to combine the ingredients and to keep the chocolate smooth. Cook until the chocolate melts. Remove the chocolate from the heat and set aside to cool.

In a large mixing bowl with a mixer on medium speed, cream the butter and the granulated sugar until light and fluffy. Add 4 egg yolks and beat for 2 minutes. Blend in the melted chocolate and the vanilla extract. In a small bowl, combine the cake flour, baking soda and salt. While continuously mixing, add 1/2 of the flour mixture and a 1/2 cup whole milk. Repeat with the remaining flour and milk until combined.

In a mixing bowl, beat the 4 egg whites on high speed until stiff peaks form. Fold the egg whites into the cake batter. Fold carefully until combined. Divide the batter evenly between the cakes pans. Bake for 20-25 minutes or until the center test clean with a toothpick. Cool the cake completely before frosting.

Coconut Pecan Frosting for German Chocolate Cake

1 1/2 cups granulated sugar
1 1/2 cups evaporated milk
3/4 cup unsalted butter
5 egg yolks, beaten
2 cups sweetened flaked coconut
1 1/2 cups chopped pecans
2 teaspoons vanilla extract

In a small saucepan over low heat, combine the granulated sugar, evaporated milk, butter and egg yolks. Stir constantly until the mixture is golden brown and thickened. Do not cook the frosting on a higher heat or the eggs will cook and look like scrambled eggs. Low heat must be used.

Remove the frosting from the heat and stir in the coconut, vanilla extract and pecans. Cool the frosting until it is thick enough to spread on the cake. Spread the frosting between the layers and on top of the cake. Let the cake sit overnight before serving.

Brandied Apple Walnut Cake

Makes a double layer 9" cake

2 cups all purpose flour
2 cups granulated sugar
2 tsp. baking powder
1 1/2 tsp. ground cinnamon
1/2 tsp. baking soda
1/4 tsp. salt
1/4 tsp. ground nutmeg
1/4 tsp. ground cloves
2 cups finely chopped peeled apples
3 beaten eggs
3/4 cup chopped walnuts
1/2 cup buttermilk
1/4 cup vegetable oil
Apple Glaze recipe below
Brandy Cream Cheese Frosting recipe below

Preheat the oven to 350°. Spray two 9" cake layer pans with non stick cooking spray. In a large mixing bowl, add the all purpose flour, granulated sugar, baking powder, cinnamon, baking soda, salt, nutmeg and cloves. Whisk until well combined.

With a spoon or whisk, stir in the apples, beaten eggs, walnuts, buttermilk and vegetable oil. Stir until well combined. Spoon the batter into the prepared cake pans. Bake for 30-40 minutes or until a toothpick inserted in the center of the cakes comes out clean. Remove the pans from the oven and cool the cake in the pans for 15 minutes. Remove the cakes from the pans and cool completely.

Apple Glaze: While the cakes are cooling, make the apple glaze. Stir constantly while making the glaze. In a sauce pan over medium heat, add 2 tablespoons granulated sugar, 2 tablespoons light brown sugar, 2 tablespoons unsalted butter, 1 tablespoon whole milk and 1 teaspoon light corn syrup. Bring the glaze to a boil. Reduce the heat to low and simmer for 3 minutes. The glaze should be reduced by half. Remove the glaze from the heat and stir in 1 tablespoon apple brandy. You can substitute apple juice for the brandy if desired. Place one cooled cake layer on a serving plate. Spoon the apple glaze over the top of the cake. Let the glaze sit for 20 minutes.

Brandy Frosting: To make the frosting, in a large mixing bowl, add 8 oz. softened cream cheese, 1/2 cup softened unsalted butter and 1 tablespoon apple brandy. Using a mixer on medium speed, mix for 3-4 minutes. The mixture should be well combined and fluffy. Turn the mixer to low and add 2 cups powdered sugar. Mix until well combined. Add 1/2 to 1 cup additional powdered sugar to make a light and fluffy frosting. The frosting should be thick, soft and spreadable.

When the glaze has set for 20 minutes, spread about 1/4 cup frosting over the cake layer. Place the remaining cake layer on top of the frosting. Spread the remaining frosting over the top and sides of the cake. Let the cake sit for 12 hours before serving.

Strawberry Angel Food Trifle

I think this is the perfect dessert for brunch. It is not too sweet or heavy. It is my favorite dessert to take to BBQ's.

Makes 8 servings

1 large baked angel food cake
8 oz. pkg. cream cheese, softened
2 cups granulated sugar
2 cups Cool Whip
1 pt. strawberries
2 tbs. cornstarch
1 cup water
4 serving size pkg. strawberry jello

Cut the angel food cake into slices. Place half of the cake slices in the bottom of an 8 x 11 brownie pan. In a mixing bowl, add the cream cheese and 1 cup granulated sugar. Beat until the cream cheese is light and fluffy. Fold in the Cool Whip.

Spread half of the Cool Whip mixture over the cake slices in the pan. Repeat with the remaining layer of cake slices. Spread the remaining Cool Whip frosting over the top of the last layer of cake slices.

In a sauce pan over medium heat, add 1 cup granulated sugar, water and cornstarch. Stir constantly and cook until the sauce thickens. Remove the pan from the heat and stir in the dry jello. Stir until the jello is dissolved.

Wash the strawberries and cut them into slices. Add the strawberry slices to the jello mixture. Stir until the strawberries are coated. Pour the strawberry mixture over the cake slices. Refrigerate until ready to serve or at least 4 hours.

Miniature Coconut Frosted Cupcakes

Serve these cupcakes at any brunch and especially Easter brunch. They are easier to make than a coconut cake. They are good and simple enough to make for any occasion. They are just the perfect bite when the afternoon sweet tooth hits.

Makes 24 mini cupcakes

2/3 cup all purpose flour
1/2 tsp. baking powder
1/8 tsp. baking soda
Pinch salt
1/4 cup unsalted butter, softened
1/2 cup granulated sugar
1/2 tsp. vanilla extract
1 egg
1/4 cup buttermilk
1 1/2 cups sweetened flaked coconut
Cream Cheese Frosting recipe below

Spray a 24 cup mini muffin tin with non stick cooking spray. Preheat the oven to 350°. In a mixing bowl, add the all purpose flour, baking powder, baking soda, 1/2 cup coconut and salt. Stir until combined and set aside for the moment.

In a mixing bowl, add the butter. Using a mixer on medium speed, beat the butter for 30 seconds. Add the granulated sugar and vanilla extract. Beat for 2 minutes. The batter should be light and fluffy. Add the egg and buttermilk. Beat for 2 minutes.

Turn the mixer to low. Slowly add the flour mixture. Mix only until combined. Spoon about 1 1/2 teaspoons batter into each muffin tin. Bake for 8-12 minutes or until the top of the cupcakes spring back when lightly touched. The cupcakes should be golden brown. Remove the pan from the oven and cool the cupcakes for 5 minutes in the pan. Remove the cupcakes and cool completely before frosting.

Cream Cheese Frosting: In a large bowl, add 4 ounces softened cream cheese and 2 tablespoons softened unsalted butter. Using a mixer on medium speed, beat for 3 minutes. The frosting should be well combined and fluffy. Add 1 teaspoon vanilla extract and 2 cups powdered sugar. Beat until the frosting is light and fluffy. Add additional powdered sugar if needed to make a thick but spreadable frosting.

Frost the cooled cupcakes. Generously sprinkle 1 cup coconut over the frosting.

Pecan Tassies

Makes 24 mini tassies

3 oz. pkg. cream cheese, softened
1/2 cup unsalted butter, softened
1 cup all purpose flour
1 cup chopped pecans
3/4 cup light brown sugar
1 tbs. unsalted butter, melted
1/4 tsp. salt
1/2 tsp. vanilla extract
1 egg

In a mixing bowl, add the cream cheese, all purpose flour and 1/2 cup softened butter. Mix thoroughly with a mixer on medium speed.

Making this crust can be tricky. You need the flour to be incorporated but you also need to mix only until combined or the crust will be tough.

Once the dough is mixed, chill the dough for 1 hour. When the dough is chilled, pinch the dough into 24 pieces. Press each piece in the cavity of a mini muffin tin. This will form the pie shell.

Preheat the oven to 350°. In a mixing bowl with a whisk, beat the brown sugar, 1 tablespoon melted butter, salt, vanilla extract and the egg. Beat until well combined. Stir in the pecans.

Spoon the filling into the pie shells. Bake for 20-25 minutes or until the filling is set and the crust is done. Remove the tassies from the oven. Let them cool for 10 minutes before removing the tassies from the pan. The tassies are delicate so be careful when removing them from the pan.

Note: I use a 1/8 measuring cup with a handle to fill the shells. It is easier and the filling does not drip all over your pan.

Choose A Flavor Tassies

Tassies are the ultimate southern dessert. They show up at baby or bridal showers, weddings, holidays and special dinners. My mother made these tassies in her bakery for 25 years. Choose any flavor you like and treat your family.

Makes 24 mini tassies

1/2 cup unsalted butter, softened
3 oz. pkg. cream cheese, softened
1 cup all purpose flour
1 recipe of fillings below

Do not over mix the dough once you add the all purpose flour. Only mix until combined. Try to mix the dough after adding the flour for less than one minute. Over mixing the dough will make the crust chewy and tough. Add the butter and cream cheese to a mixing bowl. Using a mixer on medium speed, beat for 1 minute. The batter should be well combined. Add the all purpose flour and mix only until combined. Cover the bowl and refrigerate the dough for 1 hour. The dough should be well chilled. Once the dough is mixed, chill the dough for 1 hour. When the dough is chilled, pinch the dough into 24 pieces. Press each piece in the cavity of a mini muffin tin. This will form the pie shell. Spoon 1 to 2 teaspoons of the desired filling into the pie shells. Preheat the oven to 325°. Bake for 20-30 minutes or until the filling is set and light brown. Remove the tassies from the oven and cool completely before serving.

Apricot Pecan Filling: Cover 1/3 cup diced dried apricots with boiling water. Let the apricots sit for 5 minutes in the boiling water. Drain all the water from the apricots. In a mixing bowl, add 1 egg, 3/4 cup light brown sugar and 1 tablespoon melted unsalted butter. Stir until well combined. Stir in the apricots. Fill the pastry shells and bake as directed above.

Brownie Nut Filling: In a small sauce pan over low heat, add 1/2 cup semisweet chocolate pieces and 2 tablespoons unsalted butter. Stir constantly and cook only until the chocolate melts. Remove the pan from the heat as soon as the chocolate melts. Stir in 1 egg, 1/3 cup granulated sugar and 1 teaspoon vanilla. Mix until well combined. Stir in 1/3 cup chopped pecans or peanuts. Fill the pastry shells and bake as directed above.

Cranberry Nut Filling: In a mixing bowl, add 1 egg, 3/4 cup light brown sugar, 1 tablespoon melted butter and 1 teaspoon vanilla extract. Whisk until well combined. Stir in 1/3 cup finely chopped fresh cranberries and 3 tablespoons chopped walnuts. Fill the pastry shells and bake as directed above.

Lemon Chess Filling: In a mixing bowl, add 1 egg, 1 egg yolk, 1/3 cup granulated sugar, 2 tablespoons melted unsalted butter, 1 tablespoon whole milk, 1/2 teaspoon grated lemon zest, 1 tablespoon lemon juice and 1 teaspoon cornmeal. Mix until well combined. Fill the pastry shells and bake as directed above.

Pumpkin Filling: In a mixing bowl, add 1 egg, 1/2 cup canned pumpkin, 1/4 cup granulated sugar, 1/4 cup whole milk and 1 teaspoon pumpkin pie spice. Mix until well combined. Fill the pastry shells and bake as directed above.

Fudge Peppermint Candy Brownies

Makes a 9" square pan

1 1/2 cups chocolate wafer crumbs
1/3 cup finely chopped toasted pecans
1/2 cup plus 1/3 cup unsalted butter, softened
16 chocolate covered peppermint patties
3 unsweetened chocolate squares, 1 oz. each
1 cup granulated sugar
2 eggs, beaten
1/2 tsp. vanilla extract
1/2 tsp. peppermint extract
1/2 cup all purpose flour
1/8 tsp. salt

Preheat the oven to 350°. Line a 9" square pan with aluminum foil. Make the foil large enough to leave a 1" overhang on the pan. Spray the aluminum foil with non stick cooking spray.

In a mixing bowl, add the chocolate wafer crumbs, pecans and 1/3 cup softened butter. Stir until well combined. Press the mixture into the bottom of the prepared pan. Bake for 10 minutes. Remove the pan from the oven.

Place 10 peppermint patties over the bottom of the crust. Place the patties over the crust as soon as removed from the oven.

While the crust is baking, add 1/2 cup butter and unsweetened chocolate squares to a large microwavable bowl. Microwave for 1 minute or until the chocolate and butter melt. Stir the chocolate and butter together. Stir in the granulated sugar, eggs, vanilla extract and peppermint extract. Whisk until well combined. Stir in the flour and salt. Spoon the mixture over the crust in the pan. Bake for 20-30 minutes.

Do not over bake the brownies. Check the brownies at 15 minutes and check every couple of minutes until the brownies are done. The brownies will be done when the center is set. Break the remaining 6 peppermint patties in half. Place the patties over the top of the brownies. Return the brownies to the oven for 2 minutes. Remove the brownies from the oven. Using a knife, swirl the melted peppermint patties over the top. Let the brownies cool completely. Remove the brownies from the pan using the aluminum foil sides as handles.

This brownie is very rich. Cut into small pieces and serve. I cut the brownie into 30 pieces about the size of fudge pieces.

Glazed Apple Brownies

Makes a 9 x 13 baking pan

These are very good for potlucks, brunch or barbecues. This recipe is one of my favorite non chocolate brownies.

1 cup unsalted butter, melted
1 3/4 cups granulated sugar
2 eggs
1 1/4 tsp. vanilla extract
2 cups self rising flour
1 tbs. ground cinnamon
2 cups chopped apples
1/2 cup chopped pecans
3/4 cup powdered sugar
2 tbs. hot water

Preheat the oven to 350°. Spray a 9 x 13 baking pan with non stick cooking spray. In a mixing bowl, add the butter, granulated sugar, eggs and 1 teaspoon vanilla extract. Stir until well combined.

Stir in the self rising flour, cinnamon, apples and pecans. Mix only until combined. Pour the batter into the prepared pan. Bake for 25-35 minutes or until the brownies are done. A toothpick inserted in the center should come out clean with the brownies are done.

You will cook these brownies longer than chocolate brownies. They will not be gooey like fudge brownies. Remove the brownies from the oven. Cool the brownies for 45 minutes.

While the brownies are cooling, make the glaze. In a small bowl, add the powdered sugar, 1/4 teaspoon vanilla extract and hot water. Whisk until combined. Drizzle the glaze over the cooled brownies.

Blackberry Bars

Prepare these easy bars for your next cook out.

Makes an 8" square pan

1 cup all purpose flour
3/4 cup light brown sugar
1/4 cup unsalted butter
1/2 cup sour cream
3/4 tsp. baking soda
1/4 tsp. salt
1 tsp. ground cinnamon
1/2 tsp. vanilla extract
1 cup fresh blackberries
1/2 cup powdered sugar

Preheat the oven to 350°. In a mixing bowl, add the all purpose flour, brown sugar and butter. Cut the butter into the flour and brown sugar using a pastry blender. The mixture should resemble crumbs. Press 1 1/3 cups of the mixture into the bottom of an 8" square baking pan.

Add the sour cream, baking soda, salt, ground cinnamon and vanilla extract to the remaining crumbs. Stir until well combined. Gently fold in the blackberries. Spoon the mixture over the crust in the pan.

Bake for 25-35 minutes. The bars should be set and the bottom golden. Remove the bars from the pan and cool completely before serving. Sprinkle the powdered sugar over the bars before serving.

Blueberry Pinwheel Cobbler

Cobbler is delicious anytime of the year. It is an easy dish for a potluck or barbecue.

Makes 8 servings

2 cups granulated sugar
2 cups water
1 tsp. vanilla extract
1/2 tsp. lemon juice
1/2 cup butter flavored shortening
1 1/2 cups self rising flour
1/3 cup whole milk
2 cups fresh blueberries
1/2 cup unsalted butter
Vanilla ice cream, optional

In a sauce pan over medium heat, add the granulated sugar and water. Stir constantly while making the syrup. When the sugar dissolves, stir in the vanilla extract and lemon juice. Remove the pan from the heat and set aside to cool.

In a mixing bowl, add the shortening and self rising flour. Using a pastry blender, cut the shortening into the flour. The mixture should resemble crumbs. You should still be able to see tiny pieces of shortening when done. Add the milk and stir only until the dough is moistened.

Lightly flour your work surface. Turn the dough onto your work surface. Knead the dough 5 times or until the dough holds together. Roll the dough to a 12 x 9 rectangle. Spread the blueberries over the dough. Starting with a long end, roll the dough up like a jelly roll. Seal the ends and the seam. Wet your fingers with water if needed to seal the seam and edges. With a sharp knife, cut the dough into 12 slices.

Preheat the oven to 350°. Place the butter in a 9 x 13 baking dish. Place the dish in the oven to melt the butter. Place the cobbler slices in the melted butter. Pour the syrup over the slices in the pan. Bake for 50-60 minutes. The cobbler slices should be golden brown. Remove the pan from the oven and cool for 15 minutes before serving.

Serve with a scoop of ice cream over each serving if desired.

Peppermint Stick Cookies

Makes about 2 dozen cookies

3/4 cup unsalted butter, softened
6 tbs. granulated sugar
2 cups all purpose flour
1/2 cup crushed peppermint sticks or hard peppermint candies
1 egg, separated
1 tsp. vanilla extract
24 semi sweet chocolate chips
1/4 cup granulated sugar

Preheat the oven to 350°. Place parchment paper on two cookie baking sheets.

In a large mixing bowl with the mixer set on medium speed, add the butter and 6 tablespoons granulated sugar. Beat for 3 minutes. The granulated sugar should be well incorporated into the butter. Add the egg yolk and vanilla extract. Beat for 2 minutes.

Reduce the mixer speed to low. Add the all purpose flour and mix until blended. Do not mix more than a minute or two. With a heavy spoon, stir in the crushed peppermint candies.

Roll the dough into 1" balls. In a small bowl with a whisk, beat the egg white for 2 minutes. In a small bowl, place 1/4 cup granulated sugar. Dip the top of the cookie dough balls into the egg white. Roll the top of the cookie in the granulated sugar. Place the cookie dough ball on the baking pan. Repeat until all cookies are done.

With your thumb, make a small imprint in the top of the cookie. This will allow space for the chocolate chip and also deflate the cookie slightly.

Place a chocolate chip on each cookie. Bake the cookies for 10-12 minutes or until the cookies are set. Remove the cookie sheet from the oven. Let the cookies rest for 2 minutes on the baking sheet before removing from the pan.

Gingerbread Cut Outs

Makes about 4 dozen cookies

1/2 cup vegetable shortening
1/2 cup granulated sugar
1 tsp. baking powder
1 tsp. ground ginger
1/2 tsp. baking soda
1/2 tsp. ground cinnamon
1/2 tsp. ground cloves
1 egg
1/2 cup molasses
1 tbs. vinegar
2 1/2 cups all purpose flour

The cookies will vary depending upon the size cookie cutters you use. A 2" cookie cutter will produce about 4 dozen cookies.

In a large mixing bowl, add the vegetable shortening. Beat the shortening with a mixer on medium speed for 1 minute. Add the granulated sugar, baking powder, ginger, baking soda, cinnamon and cloves. Mix for 1 minute. All the ingredients should be well combined.

Add the egg, molasses and vinegar. Mix until well combined. Reduce the mixer speed to low and add the all purpose flour. The dough will be thick and you may have to stir the all purpose flour in with a heavy spoon. Divide the dough into two equal portions. Wrap the dough in plastic wrap and refrigerate for 3 hours. The dough must be well chilled.

Preheat the oven to 375°. Spray a cookie sheet with non stick cooking spray. Work with one portion of the dough at a time. Leave the remaining dough in the refrigerator until you are ready to use it. Lightly flour your work surface. Roll the dough to about 1/8" thick. Cut out the cookies with your favorite cookie cutters. Bake for 5-8 minutes. The edges of the cookies should be light brown when ready. Cool the cookies and decorate if desired.

Orange Sugar Squares

This was my Me Maw's favorite cookie. This is a good dough for decorated cookies. Me Maw always made these cookies at Easter and Christmas. We all loved the hint of orange flavor. It is a different flavor than regular sugar cookies and always a welcome change of pace.

Drizzle the cookies with vanilla or chocolate glaze if desired.

Makes 16 cookies

2 1/2 cups all purpose flour
2 tsp. baking powder
1 tsp. salt
3/4 cup unsalted butter, softened
1 1/4 cups granulated sugar
2 eggs
1 tbs. grated orange zest

In a mixing bowl, add the all purpose flour, baking powder and salt. Stir until combined. In a separate bowl, add the butter and 1 cup granulated sugar. Using a mixer on medium speed, beat the butter and sugar for 4 minutes. The mixture should be light and fluffy. Add the eggs and orange zest. Beat for 2 minutes.

Turn the mixer to low. Slowly add the all purpose flour mixture. Mix only until combined. The dough should form and pull away from the sides of the bowl. Remove the dough from the bowl and place on a sheet of plastic wrap. Wrap the dough and chill at least 2 hours. The dough needs to be well chilled to make it easy to handle.

Preheat the oven to 400°. Lightly flour your work surface. Roll the dough out to a 16" square. Sprinkle 1/4 cup granulated sugar over the dough. Using a fluted pastry wheel, cut the cookies into 4" squares. Place the cookies on a baking sheet about 1" apart.

Bake for 6-8 minutes or until the cookies are firm. Remove the cookies from the oven and cool for 2 minutes in the pan. Remove the cookies from the baking sheet and cool completely before glazing.

Lemon Crinkles

Makes about 5 dozen

These little cookies are great for brunch, a New Year's party and especially for Easter. The lemon flavor is light enough that everyone loves them and very pretty on a cookie tray.

3/4 cup unsalted butter, softened
1 1/4 cups granulated sugar
1 egg
1/2 tsp. vanilla extract
1/2 tsp. lemon extract
1/4 cup whole milk
2 cups all purpose flour
1 tsp. baking powder
1/2 tsp. salt
1/4 tsp. baking soda
1 tbs. grated lemon zest

In a mixing bowl, add the butter and 3/4 cup granulated sugar. Using a mixer on medium speed, beat for 4 minutes. Add the egg, vanilla extract, lemon extract and milk. Beat until well combined.

Turn the mixer to low. Add the all purpose flour, baking powder, salt and baking soda. Mix only until combined. Cover the dough and chill at least 4 hours. The dough needs to be well chilled.

Preheat the oven to 350°. In a small bowl, stir together 1/2 cup granulated sugar and the lemon zest. Using about a teaspoon of cookie dough, form the dough into a ball. Roll the cookie in the sugar mixture. Place the cookies about 2" apart on an ungreased cookie sheet. Bake for 8-10 minutes. The tops should be cracked and the edges lightly browned. Remove the cookies from the oven. Cool for 1 minute on the cookie sheet. Remove the cookies from the pan and cool before serving.

Bourbon Christmas Fruit Cookies

Makes about 6 dozen

1 cup light brown sugar
1/2 cup unsalted butter, softened
4 eggs, beaten
1 tbs. whole milk
3 tsp. baking soda
3 cups all purpose flour
1 tsp. ground nutmeg
1 tsp. ground cinnamon
1 tsp. ground cloves
2 cups chopped pecans
2 oz. Kentucky bourbon
1 lb. pecan halves
8 oz. candied cherries, chopped
8 oz. candied pineapples, chopped
12 oz. golden raisins

These cookies need to be baked about 3 weeks before serving. Preheat the oven to 250°. Spray your cookie sheets with non stick cooking spray. In a mixing bowl, add the all purpose flour, baking soda, chopped pecans, cherries, pineapples and raisins. Toss to coat the fruit with the flour.

In a mixing bowl, add the butter and brown sugar. Beat with a mixer on medium speed for 3 minutes. Add the eggs, milk, bourbon, nutmeg, cinnamon and cloves. Beat for 3 minutes. Turn the mixer speed to low.

Add the flour and fruit mixture. Mix only until combined. Drop the cookies by teaspoonfuls onto your prepared baking sheets. Place a pecan half on the top of each cookie. Press the pecan half down slightly into the dough. Space the cookies about 2" apart. Bake for 12-14 minutes. Every oven cooks differently and this cookie can be tricky.

The cookie needs to be dry throughout but it should not be browned. Cook in your oven only as long as needed to dry the cookie. Cool the cookies for 1 minute on the cookie sheet before removing them from the pan. Cool the cookies completely and store in an airtight container at room temperature.

Mother's Famous Sugar Cookies

My mother made these cookies for every holiday and we decorated them for the holiday. She made thousands of these in her bakery. Her variations are listed below.

Makes about 3 dozen cookies using a 1" to 1 1/2" cookie cutter

1/2 cup unsalted butter, softened
1 cup granulated sugar
1 egg
1 tbs. whole milk
1/2 tsp. vanilla extract
1/2 tsp. salt
2 tsp. baking powder
1 3/4 cup plus 2 tbs. all purpose flour

In a mixing bowl, add the butter and granulated sugar. Beat with a mixer on medium speed for 3 minutes. Add the egg, milk and vanilla extract. Beat for 2 minutes.

Reduce the mixer speed to low. Add the salt, baking powder and all purpose flour. Mix only until combined. This will be a stiff dough. Scoop the dough onto a large piece of plastic wrap. Form the dough into a large ball. Refrigerate the dough for 8 hours but no longer than 24 hours.

You need the dough to stay chilled while working with the dough. The chilled butter in the dough is what makes the cookie flaky. Remove 1/4 of the dough at a time. Place the dough on a lightly floured work surface.

Preheat the oven to 375°. Roll the dough to a 1/4" thickness. Cut out the cookies with your favorite cookie cutters. Place the cookies on an ungreased cookie sheet. Bake for 8-10 minutes depending upon the size cookie cutter used. The bottoms of the cookies should be lightly browned when ready but the edges should not be browned. Remove the cookies from the oven and cool completely before decorating.

Chocolate Sugar Cookie: Add 2 ounces melted sweetened chocolate to the butter and sugar when mixed. Follow the recipe as directed above.

To use unsweetened cocoa powder, add 1/3 cup unsweetened cocoa when you add the flour. Follow the recipe as directed above.

Spice Sugar Cookie: Add 1/2 teaspoon of cinnamon, ground cloves, ground nutmeg and lemon zest. Add the spices when you add the flour. Follow the recipe as directed above.

Brownie Waffle Cookies

These are cute and easy to make. Kids love them!

Makes 2 dozen

1/3 cup vegetable shortening
1 oz. square unsweetened chocolate
1 egg, beaten
1/2 cup granulated sugar
2 tbs. whole milk
1/2 tsp. vanilla extract
3/4 cup all purpose flour
1/2 tsp. baking powder
1/4 tsp. salt
1 cup finely chopped pecans

In a small sauce pan over low heat, add the vegetable shortening and chocolate. Stir constantly until the chocolate melts. Remove the pan from the heat.

In a mixing bowl, add the egg, granulated sugar, milk and vanilla extract. Stir until well combined. Stir in the chocolate. Stir in the all purpose flour, baking powder, salt and 2/3 cup pecans. Mix until well blended.

Preheat your waffle iron to medium heat. Drop the cookie batter by tablespoonfuls onto the hot waffle iron. Space the cookies about 2" apart. Sprinkle the cookies lightly with the remaining pecans. Close the waffle iron and cook about 3 minutes. Check your waffle iron as each waffle iron cooks differently. They take 3 minutes on my waffle iron. Remove the cookies from the waffle iron and cool before serving.

Dust the cookies with powdered sugar or drizzle with glaze if desired.

Chocolate Cookie Ice Cream Sandwiches

These are a welcome and refreshing end to any grilled meal.

Makes 20 sandwiches

1 cup vegetable shortening
1 cup granulated sugar
1/3 cup light brown sugar
2 eggs
1 3/4 cups all purpose flour
1/3 cup unsweetened cocoa
1 tsp. baking soda
1/2 tsp. salt
1 cup semi sweet chocolate chips
1 tsp. vanilla extract
1/2 gallon vanilla ice cream

Preheat the oven to 375°. In a mixing bowl, add the vegetable shortening, granulated sugar and brown sugar. Using a mixer on medium speed, beat for 4 minutes. The mixture should be light and fluffy.

Add the eggs and beat for 2 minutes. The eggs should be well combined. In a separate bowl, add the all purpose flour, cocoa, baking soda and salt. Turn the mixer to low. Slowly add the dry ingredients to the wet ingredients. Mix only until combined. Turn the mixer off. Using a heavy spoon, stir in the chocolate chips and vanilla extract.

Shape the dough into 1 1/2" balls. Place the cookies on an ungreased cookie sheet. With the palm of your hand, gently press the cookies down to a 2 1/2" diameter. Bake for 6-8 minutes or until the cookies are soft but firm. Remove the cookies from the oven and cool the cookies for 1 minute on the cookie sheet.

Remove the cookies from the cookie sheet and cool completely. When ready to serve, place 1/2 cup scoop vanilla ice cream on half of the cookies. Top the ice cream with the remaining cookies. Press the sandwiches gently together and serve. You can make the cookies ahead of time and keep frozen until ready to serve. Store the cookies in an airtight container in the freezer.

Oatmeal Raisin Ice Cream Sandwiches

Makes 12 sandwiches

1 cup unsalted butter, softened
1 cup light brown sugar
1/2 cup granulated sugar
2 eggs
1 tsp. vanilla extract
1 1/2 cups all purpose flour
1 tsp. baking soda
1 tsp. ground cinnamon
1/2 tsp. salt
3 cups old fashioned oats
1 cup raisins
1 quart vanilla ice cream

Preheat the oven to 350°. In a mixing bowl, add the butter, brown sugar and granulated sugar. Using a mixer on medium speed, beat for 3 minutes. Add the eggs and vanilla extract. Beat for 2 minutes.

Turn the mixer to low. Add the all purpose flour, baking soda, cinnamon and salt. Mix only until combined. Turn the mixer off. Using a heavy spoon, stir in the oats and raisins. Drop the cookie dough by tablespoonfuls onto an ungreased baking sheet. You should have 24 cookies.

Bake for 10-12 minutes or until the cookies are light golden brown. Remove the cookies from the oven and cool the cookies for 1 minute on the cookie sheet. Remove the cookies from the cookie sheet and cool before using.

Place a scoop of ice cream on 12 of the cookies. Place the remaining cookies over the ice cream. Using the palm of your hand, gently press the cookies together to help spread the ice cream. Wrap the cookies in plastic wrap. Place the cookies in a freezer bag and freeze until ready to use.

Blackberry & Cream Parfaits

These are perfect for barbecues.

Makes 8 servings

3 oz. pkg. blackberry flavored jello
1 cup boiling water
1/2 cup orange juice
8 oz. pkg. cream cheese, softened
3 tbs. granulated sugar
8 oz. container Cool Whip
2 cups fresh blackberries

In a mixing bowl, add the jello and boiling water. Stir until the jello dissolves. Add the orange juice and stir until combined. Set the bowl aside for the moment.

In a mixing bowl, add the cream cheese and granulated sugar. Using a mixer on medium speed, beat for 3 minutes. The mixture should be light and fluffy. Turn the mixer to low. Slowly add the jello mixture. Beat until smooth.

Place the bowl in the refrigerator and chill until the jello is slightly thickened. The jello should be the consistency of jelly. When the jello is ready, gently fold in the Cool Whip.

Layer the jello mixture and blackberries in tall parfait glasses. Alternate layers of the jello mixture with blackberries. Chill the dessert until ready to serve.

Lemon Creme Parfaits

Makes 6 servings

4 serving size pkg. lemon cook & serve pudding mix
1 1/2 cups water
1/2 cup granulated sugar
1 cup unsweetened pineapple juice
2 egg yolks, beaten
1 cup whipped cream or Cool Whip
1 pint strawberries, cleaned and hulled
6 ladyfingers, halved lengthwise and crosswise

In a sauce pan over low heat, add the pudding mix, sugar, pineapple juice, egg yolks and water. Stir constantly while making the pudding. Cook until the pudding begins to thicken. Remove the pan from the heat as soon as the pudding thickens.

Let the pudding cool for 10 minutes. Gently fold in the whipped cream. Place half of the pudding in the bottom of 6 parfait glasses. Reserve 6 strawberries for garnish. Divide the remaining strawberries between the 6 glasses. Cover the strawberries with the remaining pudding. Place the ladyfingers around the edge of each parfait glass. Place the reserved strawberries on top. Place the parfaits in the refrigerator at least 2 hours before serving.

Heavenly Cream Squares

Makes a 9" square pan

1 3/4 cups vanilla wafer crumbs
1/2 cup chopped pecans
1/2 cup unsalted butter, melted
4 serving size pkg. vanilla instant pudding mix
1 3/4 cups whole milk
1/4 tsp. rum flavoring
8 oz. pkg. cream cheese, softened.

In a 9" square pan, add the vanilla wafer crumbs, pecans and melted butter. Stir until the ingredients are well combined. Reserve 1/2 cup of the crumbs and set aside for the moment.

Press the remaining crumbs into the bottom of the pan to form a crust. In a mixing bowl, add the vanilla pudding mix and milk. Whisk until the pudding begins to thicken. Add the rum flavoring and cream cheese. Whisk together until the cream cheese is well blended. Spoon the mixture over the vanilla wafer crust. Sprinkle the remaining crumbs across the top of the dessert.

Refrigerate for 4 hours before serving.

Chocolate Dessert Shells

Fill these shells with ice cream, fruit or pudding for a decadent and different dessert.

Makes 8 shells

2/3 cup semisweet chocolate chips
2 cups sweetened flaked coconut
1/2 cup chopped pecans

In a sauce pan over low heat, add the chocolate chips. Stir constantly until the chocolate melts. Remove the pan from the heat and stir in the coconut and pecans.

Place 8 paper cupcake liners in 8 muffin cups. Spoon the mixture on the bottom and up the sides of the cupcake liner. Press to form if necessary. Chill the shells in the refrigerator until firm.

When ready to serve, remove the paper liner from the dessert shell. Fill with ice cream, pudding or fruit to serve.

Bourbon Balls

It would not be the holidays unless we made bourbon balls!

Makes 2 dozen

1 cup finely crushed vanilla wafers
1 cup grated pecans
1 1/2 cups powdered sugar
2 tbs. unsweetened cocoa
1 1/2 tbs. light corn syrup
2 oz. Kentucky bourbon

In a mixing bowl, add the bourbon and corn syrup. Whisk until well combined. Add the vanilla wafers, pecans, 1 cup powdered sugar and unsweetened cocoa. Stir until well blended. Form the candy into small balls with your hands. Use about 1 tablespoon of the candy for each ball.

Roll the balls in the remaining 1/2 cup powdered sugar. Store in an airtight container.

Me Maw's Divinity

Do not make this candy on a rainy or very humid day. It will not set up.

Makes about 5 dozen candies

5 cups granulated sugar
1 cup light corn syrup
1 cup water
3 egg whites
2 tsp. vanilla extract
2 cups pecan halves

I am going to start by saying that divinity is not hard to make, but you have to follow the directions carefully. Read the recipe thoroughly and have everything ready to go as you will not have time to do prep work once you start.

Line three large baking sheets with waxed paper. In a large heavy sauce pan over medium heat, add the granulated sugar, light corn syrup and water. Stir constantly until the sugar dissolves. Do not stir once the sugar is completely dissolved. The candy will be clear like water. Put a candy thermometer on the pan and cook to 250°.

While the candy is cooking, beat the egg whites in a large mixing bowl until you have stiff peaks. Once the candy has reached 250°, slowly start pouring the candy liquid into the egg whites. Beat on medium to high speed with the mixer while you are pouring the candy. After you have poured all the candy mixture, add the vanilla extract to the egg whites. Continue beating until it begins to thicken. This will take 5-6 minutes.

You have to work fast once the divinity starts to thicken. Scoop out a teaspoon of divinity and use another teaspoon to scrape the candy off the spoon onto the waxed paper. Once you have all the divinity scooped onto waxed paper, top each piece with a pecan half. Gently press the pecan half into the divinity. Cool completely before serving.

Peanut Butter Easter Eggs

My mother made these eggs every Easter. Our Easter baskets were filled with them, fudge bunnies and large decorated sugar cookies. We were in heaven!

Makes about 18 small eggs

1 1/2 cups unsalted butter, softened
3/4 cup crunchy peanut butter
1 1/2 tbs. light corn syrup
1/2 tsp. vanilla extract
1 1/2 to 2 lbs. powdered sugar
12 oz. pkg. chocolate candy coating

In a mixing bowl, add the butter, peanut butter, corn syrup and vanilla extract. Using a mixer on medium speed, beat until smooth and fluffy. In my mixer, it takes about 3 minutes.

Turn the mixer to low. Stir in 1 cup powdered sugar at a time. Keep the mixer running while adding the powdered sugar. Keep adding the powdered sugar until the mixture is no longer sticky and you can handle the filling easily.

Form each portion into an egg shape. The shape should be oval and flat on the bottom. Place the candies on waxed paper and cover the candies loosely with paper towels. Let the candies dry for 12 hours at room temperature.

Melt the candy coating in the microwave or over a double boiler. Using a fork, dip each egg candy into the chocolate coating. Place the candies on waxed paper. Refrigerate the candies for 15 minutes or until the chocolate is set.

Store the candies in the refrigerator up to 4 weeks. Decorate the eggs if desired.

If you would like to make large eggs, form the candy into 6 eggs. Follow the directions as stated above.

Cream Cheese Fudge

Makes an 8" square pan

1 tbs. unsalted butter, softened
4 squares unsweetened chocolate, 1 oz. each
6 oz. cream cheese, softened
4 cups powdered sugar
1/2 tsp. vanilla extract
1 cup chopped pecans
Pecan halves, optional

Grease an 8" square pan with butter. Over the top of a double boiler, add the chocolate squares. The heat for the double boiler should be reduced to low after the water boils. Stir constantly until the chocolate melts. Remove the pan from the heat once the chocolate melts.

In a mixing bowl, add the cream cheese and powdered sugar. Beat with a mixer on medium speed until well combined and smooth. Stir in the melted chocolate and vanilla extract. Beat until well combined. Add the pecans and beat until combined.

Press the fudge into the buttered pan. Place the pan in the refrigerator and chill until firm. Cut into small pieces and top each piece with a pecan half if desired.

Chocolate Caramel Fudge

Makes a 9" square pan

3 cups light brown sugar
3 tbs. all purpose flour
1 1/2 cups molasses
3/4 cup plus 1 tbs. unsalted butter
6 squares unsweetened chocolate, 1 oz. each square
1 1/2 cups whole milk
1 1/2 tsp. vanilla extract
1/3 cup sliced toasted almonds

Grease a 9" square pan with 1 tablespoon butter. In a heavy sauce pan over medium heat, add the brown sugar, all purpose flour, molasses and 3/4 cup butter. Bring the candy to a boil. Stir constantly and cook for 5 minutes.

Add the chocolate and milk to the pan. Stir until the chocolate melts. Stir frequently and cook until the fudge reaches 235° on a candy thermometer. Remove the pan from the heat and stir in the vanilla extract.

Pour the fudge into the prepared pan. Sprinkle the almonds over the fudge. Refrigerate the fudge for 12 hours. Cut into small pieces and serve. Store the fudge in an airtight container in the refrigerator.

Pistachio Fudge

Makes an 8" square pan

4 cups granulated sugar
2 cups whole milk
1/2 cup plus 1 tbs. unsalted butter
1/4 tsp. salt
1 tsp. vanilla extract
1/4 cup finely chopped roasted pistachios
Candied red and green cherries

Grease an 8" square pan with 1 tablespoon butter. In a large sauce pan over low heat, add the granulated sugar, milk, 1/2 cup butter and salt. Stir constantly while making the fudge. When the sugar dissolves, increase the heat to medium. Cook until the fudge reaches 235° on a candy thermometer. Remove the pan from the heat and cool the fudge to 110°.

When the fudge has cooled to 110°, stir in the pistachios and vanilla extract. Using a wooden spoon, beat for 3 minutes or until the fudge thickens and begins to lose the glossy shine. Pour the fudge into the prepared pan.

Score the fudge into pieces. Do not cut the pieces but just score the top. Place a candied cherry on each piece. Cool the fudge until firm or about 12 hours.

Cherry Nut Fudge

Makes an 8" square pan

3 2/3 cups powdered sugar
1/2 cup unsweetened cocoa
1/2 cup plus 1 tbs. unsalted butter
3 tbs. whole milk
1 tbs. vanilla extract
1/2 cup chopped candied cherries
1/2 cup chopped pecans

In a mixing bowl, stir together the powdered sugar and cocoa. Set aside for the moment. Grease an 8" square pan with 1 tablespoon butter.

In a sauce pan over low heat, add 1/2 cup butter and milk. Stir constantly and cook until the butter melts. Remove the pan from the heat and stir in the powdered sugar and cocoa. Stir until the fudge is smooth.

Stir in the vanilla extract, cherries and pecans. Spoon the fudge into the prepared pan. Refrigerate until firm. Cut into small pieces and serve.

Double Peanut Fudge

Makes an 8" square pan

2 cups granulated sugar
2/3 cup whole milk
1 cup marshmallow creme
1 cup creamy peanut butter
6 oz. pkg. semi sweet chocolate chips
1 tsp. vanilla extract
1/2 cup coarsely chopped peanuts
1 tbs. unsalted butter

Grease an 8" square pan with butter. In a sauce pan over medium heat, add the granulated sugar and milk. Stir occasionally and cook until the temperature reaches 234° on a candy thermometer. Remove the pan from the heat.

Stir in the marshmallow creme, peanut butter, chocolate chips and vanilla extract. Stir until well blended and the fudge is smooth. Fold in the peanuts and spoon the fudge into the prepared pan. Cool until the fudge is firm. Cut into small pieces and serve.

Chocolate Peanut Butter Fudge

Makes a 9" square pan

2 1/2 cups granulated sugar
1/4 cup unsweetened cocoa
1 cup whole milk
1 tbs. light corn syrup
1/2 cup plus 1 tbs. unsalted butter
1/2 cup peanut butter
1 cup chopped pecans
2 tsp. vanilla extract

Grease a 9" square pan with 1 tablespoon butter. In a large heavy sauce pan over medium heat, add the granulated sugar, cocoa, milk and light corn syrup. Stir constantly until the sugar dissolves. Add 2 tablespoons butter. Stir until the butter melts.

Place a lid on the sauce pan and bring the fudge to a boil. Boil for 3 minutes. Remove the cover but do not stir. Cook until the fudge reaches 234° on a candy thermometer. Remove the pan from the heat and add the remaining butter, peanut butter, pecans and vanilla extract. Do not stir!

Let the fudge cool for 10 minutes. With a heavy spoon, beat the fudge until combined and the fudge has thickened. Spoon the fudge into the prepared pan. Cool the fudge for 6 hours at room temperature before slicing.

Store the fudge in an airtight container at room temperature for no more than 1 week. Refrigerate up to 2 months.

Old Fashioned Millionaires

My mother made these by the hundreds every Christmas. To this day, I still love them and make them for Christmas and Easter.

Makes about 36 candies

14 oz. pkg. caramels, unwrapped
3-4 tbs. whole milk
2 cups pecan pieces
2 tbs. unsalted butter
1 tbs. vegetable shortening
12 oz. pkg. semisweet chocolate chips

Spread out a large sheet of waxed paper. Butter the waxed paper. Butter well or the candies will stick and be a mess to remove from the waxed paper. In a heavy sauce pan over low heat, add the caramels and milk. Stir constantly and heat only until the caramels melt. Stir in the pecans.

Drop the candies by tablespoonfuls onto the waxed paper. Let the candies sit at room temperature until firm. When the candies are firm, make the chocolate coating.

In a sauce pan over low heat, add the chocolate chips and vegetable shortening. Stir constantly until the chocolate and shortening melt. Using a fork, dip each candy into the chocolate coating. Place the dipped candy on a sheet of waxed paper to cool.

Store the candies in the refrigerator when cool in an airtight container.

Chocolate Cream Drops

Makes about 8 dozen candies

2 lbs. powdered sugar
1 1/2 cups sweetened condensed milk
1/2 cup unsalted butter, melted
1 tsp. vanilla extract
2 cups chopped pecans
1 cup flaked coconut
12 oz. pkg. semisweet chocolate chips
3 tbs. vegetable shortening

In a mixing bowl, add the powdered sugar, sweetened condensed milk, butter, vanilla extract, pecans and coconut. Using a heavy spoon, stir until well combined. Roll the mixture into 1" balls. Place the balls on a baking sheet and chill for 2 hours.

When the candy has chilled, add the chocolate chips and vegetable shortening to a heavy sauce pan. Place the pan over low heat. Stir constantly until the chocolate and shortening melts. Remove the candies from the refrigerator.

Using a fork, dip each ball into the melted chocolate. Place the candies on waxed paper to cool. Store the cooled candies in an airtight container in the refrigerator.

Peanut Butter Creams

Makes about 6 dozen

1/4 cup powdered sugar
1/2 cup sweetened condensed milk
1 cup creamy peanut butter
6 oz. pkg. semisweet chocolate chips
1/2 to 1 cup chocolate sprinkles

In a mixing bowl, add the powdered sugar, sweetened condensed milk, peanut butter and chocolate chips. Stir until well combined. Chill the candy until firm.

When the candy is firm, use about a teaspoon of the candy and roll into a 3/4" ball. Place the chocolate sprinkles in a small bowl. Roll each candy in the chocolate sprinkles. Repeat until all the candies are done. Chill the candies until firm. Store in an airtight container in the refrigerator.

Kentucky Colonels

Makes about 6 dozen

1/2 cup unsalted butter, softened
2 tbs. sweetened condensed milk
1/3 cup plus 2 tsp. bourbon
7 1/2 cups powdered sugar
1/2 cup finely chopped pecans
6 oz. pkg. semisweet chocolate chips
1 tbs. vegetable shortening
Pecan halves

In a large mixing bowl, add the butter, sweetened condensed milk, bourbon and powdered sugar. Using your hands, mix until well combined. Knead the dough until smooth and it no longer sticks to your hands. This takes considerable kneading. Knead in the chopped pecans.

Roll the candy mixture into 1" balls. Place the balls on a cookie sheet. In a sauce pan over low heat, add the chocolate chips and vegetable shortening. Stir constantly until the chocolate and shortening melt. Using a fork, dip each candy in the chocolate. Gently press a pecan half on top of each candy. Place the dipped candies on a sheet of wax paper to dry.

Chocolate Brittle

Makes about 4 lbs.

2 cups plus 2 tbs. unsalted butter (no substitutions)
2 cups granulated sugar
1/4 cup plus 2 tbs. water
12 milk chocolate candy bars, unwrapped, about 1 oz. each
3 cups chopped pecans

In a large sauce pan over low heat, add 2 cups butter, granulated sugar and water. Stir occasionally and cook until a candy thermometer reaches 300°.

While the candy is cooking, grease two 12" pizza pans with 2 tablespoons butter. Remove the pan from the heat when the candy is ready and pour the candy onto the pizza pans. Spread the candy to smooth if needed.

In a sauce pan over low heat, add the candy bars. Stir constantly until the chocolate melts. Spread the chocolate over the candy in the pans. Sprinkle the pecans over the chocolate. Gently press the pecans into the chocolate. Cool until firm. Break the candy into pieces and store in an airtight container.

Strawberry Christmas Candies

Makes about 24 strawberries

Granny made these every Christmas. They are super rich! I loved them as a kid and I still love them today.

2 pkgs. 3 oz. size strawberry jello
3/4 cup sweetened condensed milk
1/2 tsp. vanilla extract
1 cup sweetened flaked coconut, finely chopped
1 cup ground pecans
Red colored sugar
1 can green decorator frosting with a leaf tip

The red in the jello and sugar will stain your hands. I highly recommend you wear latex gloves while preparing this candy.

In a mixing bowl, add the jello, sweetened condensed milk, vanilla extract, coconut and pecans. Using your hands, mix until well combined. Use about a tablespoon of the candy mixture and form the candy into strawberries with your fingers.

Roll the strawberries in the red colored sugar. Place the strawberries on a sheet of waxed paper to dry. Use the green icing with a leaf tip and form two leaves on each strawberry. Store the strawberries in the refrigerator in an airtight container.

You can use different jello flavors to make different fruits. Use your imagination and you will be surprised what you will create. Use orange jello and form the candy into small oranges, lemon jello and create small lemons, lime jello for limes, grape jello for grapes and use the cherry jello to create small apples. Use a whole clove for the apple and grape stems.

Potato Candy

This candy is a southern favorite that is always on my holiday table.

Makes about 36-40 pieces

1 medium potato
4 to 6 cups powdered sugar
1-2 cups creamy peanut butter

Boil the potato in the skin until the potato is tender in a pan of water. Remove the potato from the water and let it cool completely. Remove the skin from the potato.

In a mixing bowl, mash the cold potato until smooth. Stir in 3 cups powdered sugar. Depending on the moisture in the potato, you may need to add more powdered sugar. Add enough powdered sugar until you have semi stiff dough.
Liberally sprinkle powdered sugar on a work surface. Using a rolling pin, roll out the dough into the shape of a rectangle. You want the dough to be about 1/4" thick. Spread the peanut butter all over the dough.

Some people like a lot of peanut butter and some don't. Use both cups of peanut butter if you like it. Starting with the long side, roll the dough up like a cinnamon roll. Be sure to seal all the sides and ends. You can dab the ends and sides with a touch of warm water to seal. Wrap the roll in plastic wrap and refrigerate overnight. Slice into 1/4" thick slices when ready to serve.

This will keep for 3-4 weeks covered in the refrigerator.

Southern Pralines

Makes about 18 candies

2 cups light brown sugar
1 cup evaporated milk
1 tsp. vanilla extract
1 cup granulated sugar
2 tbs. unsalted butter
1 1/2 cups pecans

In a medium size sauce pan, add the brown sugar, evaporated milk, granulated sugar and the butter. Stir the candy constantly until it begins to boil. Do not stir once it boils. Cook until it reaches soft ball stage or about 236° on a candy thermometer. Remove the pan from the heat and beat with a whisk or a mixer until it begins to cool and thicken. This will thicken quickly. Stir in the vanilla extract and the pecans. Drop by teaspoonfuls onto buttered waxed paper. Cool completely before serving.

Be certain to butter your waxed paper. If you skip this step, the pralines will stick to the waxed paper and you will have a terrible time trying to get them off the waxed paper.

8 BRUNCH

Brunch doesn't have to be a special occasion. I fix brunch every weekend for the family. After a lazy morning, everyone is ready to eat. You don't have to serve fancy foods.

Fix your family favorite recipes and enjoy the time spent with family. I have included several of our favorite brunch recipes. Some of the recipes can be made ahead and baked when ready. This also allows you time to enjoy your guest.

Sausage Pie

Makes 12 servings

2 unbaked 9" pie crust
1 lb. pork sausage, browned & crumbled
6 tbs. chopped green onion
8 eggs, beaten
4 cups light whipping cream
1 1/2 tsp. salt
1/2 tsp. granulated sugar
1/4 tsp. cayenne pepper

Preheat the oven to 425°. Place each of the unbaked pie shells into a 9" pie plate. Place half of the sausage and green onions in each pie plate. In a mixing bowl, combine the eggs, whipping cream, salt, granulated sugar and cayenne pepper. Pour half of the egg mixture into each pie plate.

Bake for 15 minutes at 425°. Reduce the heat to 300° and bake about 30-40 minutes or until the center of the pies are set. Remove the pies from the oven. Let the pies cool for 10 minutes before serving.

Apple Brunch Strata

Makes 8 servings

8 oz. ground pork sausage
4 cups cubed French bread
2 cups peeled and diced apples
1/4 cup sliced green onions
1/3 cup sliced black olives
1 1/2 cups shredded sharp cheddar cheese
2 cups whole milk
8 eggs
2 tsp. spicy brown mustard
1/2 tsp. salt
1/4 tsp. black pepper

In a skillet over medium heat, add the sausage. Stir frequently and break the sausage into crumbles as it cooks. Cook the sausage for 7-8 minutes or until the sausage is done. Remove the sausage from the skillet and drain on paper towels.

Spray a 9 x 13 baking dish with non stick cooking spray. Place half of the bread cubes in the pan. Spoon the sausage over the bread. Place the apples, green onions, olives and cheddar cheese over the sausage. Place the remaining bread over the top of the dish.

In a mixing bowl, add the eggs, milk, mustard, salt and black pepper. Whisk until well combined. Pour the eggs over the bread in the pan. Cover the pan with aluminum foil. Refrigerate at least 4 hours but no more than 12 hours.

Preheat the oven to 350°. Bake covered for 45 minutes. Remove the foil and bake for 15 minutes or until the strata is set. Remove the dish from the oven and cool for 10 minutes before serving.

Overnight Veggie Sausage Strata

Makes a 9 x 13 baking pan

2 lbs. ground Italian sausage
2 green bell peppers, chopped
1 onion, chopped
8 eggs
2 cups whole milk
2 tsp. salt
2 tsp. black pepper
2 tsp. stone ground mustard
12 slices bread, cut into 1/2" pieces
10 oz. pkg. frozen chopped spinach, thawed and all moisture removed
2 cups shredded Swiss cheese
2 cups shredded cheddar cheese
1 zucchini, cut into 1/4" thick slices

In a large skillet over medium heat, add the sausage, green bell peppers and onion. Stir frequently and break the sausage into crumbles as it cooks. Drain off all the excess grease from the pan.

In a large bowl, add the eggs, milk, salt, black pepper and mustard. Whisk until well blended. Stir in the sausage with vegetables, bread, spinach, Swiss cheese, cheddar cheese and zucchini. Pour the mixture into a 9 x 13 baking dish. Cover the dish with aluminum foil. Refrigerate at least 8 hours but not more than 12 hours.

Remove the strata from the refrigerator and let it sit at room temperature for 30 minutes. Preheat the oven to 350°. Do not remove the aluminum foil. Place the strata in the oven and bake for 40 minutes. Remove the aluminum foil and bake for 30-40 minutes or until the center of the strata is set and done. A knife inserted in the center of the casserole should come out clean when ready. Remove the casserole from the oven and cool for 5 minutes before serving.

Three Cheese Quiche

Makes 6 servings

This quiche makes its own crust as it bakes.

2 tsp. unsalted butter, softened
2 tbs. grated Parmesan cheese
2 cups shredded cheddar cheese
1 cup shredded Swiss cheese
2 eggs
3/4 cup whole milk
3/4 cup all purpose flour
1/2 tsp. salt
1/8 tsp. black pepper

Preheat the oven to 425°. Grease a 9" pie pan with the butter. Sprinkle 1 tablespoon Parmesan cheese over the pie pan. In a small bowl, combine the cheddar cheese and Swiss cheese. Sprinkle the cheeses over the pie pan.

In a mixing bowl, add the eggs and milk. Whisk until well combined. Add 1/4 cup all purpose flour and whisk to combine. Add another 1/4 cup all purpose flour and whisk to combine. Add the remaining all purpose flour, salt and black pepper. Whisk until well combined. The mixture should resemble heavy cream. Slowly pour the egg mixture over the cheese. Sprinkle the remaining tablespoon Parmesan cheese over the top. Bake for 30-40 minutes or until the quiche is set, browned and bubbly. Remove the quiche from the oven and cool for 10 minutes before serving.

Spinach Mushroom Breakfast Casserole

Makes a 9 x 13 baking dish

3 cups frozen tater tots
1 lb. ground pork sausage
4 eggs
10.75 oz. can cream of mushroom soup
10 oz. pkg. frozen spinach, thawed and drained
1/2 cup diced cooked mushrooms
1 cup shredded sharp cheddar cheese
1 cup shredded Monterey Jack cheese
1/4 tsp. dry mustard
Salt and black pepper to taste

In a skillet over medium heat, add the sausage. Stir frequently and break the sausage into crumbles as it cooks. Cook the sausage for 7-8 minutes or until the sausage is done and no longer pink. Drain the excess grease from the sausage.

Preheat the oven to 450°. Place the tater tots in the bottom of a 9 x 13 baking dish. Bake the tater tots for 10 minutes. Remove the pan from the oven. Sprinkle the sausage over the tater tots.

In a mixing bowl, add the eggs, cream of mushroom soup, spinach, mushrooms, cheddar cheese, Monterey Jack cheese and dry mustard. Whisk until well combined. Season with salt and black pepper to taste. Pour the mixture over the tater tots and sausage. Bake for 35-40 minutes or until the center of the casserole is set. Remove the casserole from the oven and cool for 10 minutes before serving.

Parmesan Omelet with Cheddar Sauce

Makes 4 servings

8 egg yolks
8 egg whites
1/2 cup water
1/2 cup grated Parmesan cheese
2 tbs. unsalted butter
4 tsp. unsalted butter
4 tsp. all purpose flour
3/4 cup whole milk
3/4 cup shredded cheddar cheese
Salt and black pepper to season.

Preheat the oven to 325°. In a mixing bowl, add the egg whites. Using a mixer on medium speed, beat the egg whites until stiff peaks form. Set the egg whites aside for the moment,

In a separate mixing bowl, add the egg yolks and water. Beat the egg yolks and water with a mixer on medium speed for 4 minutes or until the yolks are lemon colored. Gently fold in the beaten egg whites. Season with salt and black pepper as desired.

In a 10" oven proof skillet over medium heat, add 2 tablespoons butter. When the butter melts and begins to sizzle, add the egg mixture. Sprinkle the Parmesan cheese over the eggs. Cook about 5 minutes or until the bottom is golden and the top slightly puffed. Remove the pan from the heat and place in the skillet in the oven. Cook the omelet for 10-12 minutes or until a knife inserted off center comes out clean.

While the omelet is cooking, make the cheese sauce. In a sauce pan over low heat, add 4 teaspoons butter. When the butter melts, stir in the all purpose flour. Stir constantly and add the milk. Cook until the sauce thickens and bubbles. Stir in the cheese and cook only until the cheese melts. Remove the pan from the heat and season to taste with salt and black pepper. Remove the omelet from the oven when done and serve the cheese sauce over the omelet.

Pear Almond Quesadillas

Makes 6 servings

2 ripe pears, peeled and thinly sliced
1 tbs. unsalted butter
1 1/2 cups shredded Swiss cheese
6 flour tortillas, 8" size
1/3 cup sliced toasted almonds

In a skillet over medium heat, add the butter. When the butter melts, add the pears. Stir occasionally and cook the pears for 3 minutes. The pears should begin to soften. Remove the pears from the skillet and drain on paper towels.

Sprinkle 1/4 cup Swiss cheese over one half of the tortillas. Place the pear slices over the cheese. Sprinkle the almonds over the pears. Fold the other half of the tortilla over the pears and cheese.

Place a large skillet on the stove over medium high heat. Heat the skillet for 2 minutes. Reduce the heat to medium and place 2 tortillas at a time in the skillet. Cook for 1-2 minutes per side or until the cheese is melted and the pears hot. Remove the quesadillas from the skillet and cook the remaining tortillas.

To keep the tortillas warm, preheat the oven to 300°. Place the cooked tortillas in the oven to keep warm while you cook the remaining tortillas.

You can also serve the quesadillas as an appetizer. Cut each tortilla into 3 wedges. This will give you 18 appetizer servings.

Apple Pancakes with Cider Sauce

Makes 12 pancakes

2 cups Bisquick
1/2 tsp. ground cinnamon
1 egg, beaten
1 1/3 cups whole milk
3/4 cup shredded apple
Cider Sauce recipe below

In a mixing bowl, add the Bisquick, cinnamon, egg, milk and apple. Whisk until well blended. Heat a griddle or skillet over medium heat. Spray the griddle or skillet with non stick cooking spray if desired. Use about 1/4 cup pancake batter for each pancake.

Cook for 1-2 minutes per side or until the pancakes are puffed and golden brown.

Cider Sauce: In a sauce pan over medium heat, add 1/2 cup granulated sugar, 1 tablespoon cornstarch, 1/4 teaspoon ground cinnamon, 1/4 teaspoon ground nutmeg, 1 cup apple cider or apple juice and 1 tablespoon lemon juice. Stir constantly until the sauce boils. Cook for 1 minute after the sauce boils. Remove the pan from the heat and stir in 2 tablespoons butter.

Island Pancakes

Makes 20 pancakes

2 cups buttermilk
2 tsp. baking soda
4 eggs, beaten
2 tbs. melted unsalted butter
1 cup mashed ripe bananas
2 cups all purpose flour
2 tbs. granulated sugar
1/2 tsp. salt
Maple syrup, honey, butter and sweetened coconut for toppings

In a mixing bowl, add the buttermilk, eggs, bananas and butter. Stir until well blended. Stir in the baking soda, all purpose flour, granulated sugar and salt. Mix only until combined. Let the batter rest while you heat the griddle.

Spray your griddle with non stick cooking spray if desired. Spoon 1/4 cup batter per pancake on a hot griddle. The griddle should be about 350°. Cook the pancakes for 1-2 minutes or until the tops are covered with bubbles and the edges golden brown. Flip the pancakes over and cook about 1 minute on the other side.

Remove the pancakes from the griddle and serve with the above toppings.

Orange Yogurt Pancakes

Makes 16 pancakes

These are delicious pancakes served with strawberries and whipped cream.

1 1/4 cups Bisquick
1 tbs. granulated sugar
3/4 cup plain yogurt
1/3 cup orange juice
1/2 tsp. grated orange zest
1 egg, beaten
2 tbs. unsalted butter, melted
1 cup sliced strawberries
1 cup blueberries
1 1/2 cups whipped cream
1 cup orange yogurt, optional

In a mixing bowl, add the Bisquick, granulated sugar, plain yogurt, orange juice, orange zest, egg and melted butter. Whisk until well combined. Let the batter rest while the griddle heats up.

Spray your griddle with non stick cooking spray if desired. Spoon 1/4 cup batter per pancake on a hot griddle. The griddle should be about 350°. Cook the pancakes for 1-2 minutes or until the tops are covered with bubbles and the edges golden brown. Flip the pancakes over and cook about 1 minute on the other side.

Serve the pancakes with strawberries, blueberries and whipped cream. I like to drizzle orange yogurt over the berries.

Southern Waffles

Makes sixteen 4" waffles

1 1/4 cups self rising flour
3/4 cup self rising cornmeal
1/2 tsp. baking powder
1 tbs. granulated sugar
3 eggs, separated
1 cup buttermilk
3/4 cup whole milk
1/4 cup plus 2 tbs. melted unsalted butter

In a mixing bowl, add the egg whites. Using a mixer on medium speed, beat the egg whites until stiff peaks form. Set the egg whites aside for the moment.

In a separate mixing bowl, add the self rising flour, cornmeal, baking powder and granulated sugar. Stir until combined. In a separate bowl, add the egg yolks, buttermilk, milk and butter. Whisk until combined. Add to the dry ingredients. Mix only until the batter is moistened. Let the batter rest while the waffle iron heats. The waffles will be fluffier if the batter is allowed to rest at least 3 minutes.

Preheat your waffle iron. Gently fold the egg whites into the waffle batter. Spoon the batter onto the hot waffle iron. Cook for 3-4 minutes or until the waffles are done and golden brown. Cook according to your waffle maker's instructions.

Serve with your favorite toppings.

Pecan Waffles

Makes about twelve 4" waffles

1 3/4 cups all purpose flour
2 tsp. baking powder
1/2 tsp. salt
2 eggs, separated
1 1/4 cups whole milk
1/2 cup vegetable oil
1/2 cup plus 1 tbs. chopped pecans
Butter and syrup for toppings

In a mixing bowl, add the egg whites. Using a mixer on medium speed, beat the egg whites until stiff peaks form. Set the egg whites aside for the moment.

In a mixing bowl, add the all purpose flour, baking powder, pecans and salt. Whisk until combined. In a separate bowl, add the egg yolks, milk and vegetable oil. Whisk until combined. Add to the dry ingredients. Mix only until the batter is moistened. Gently fold in the egg whites. Let the batter rest while the waffle iron heats. The waffles will be fluffier if the batter is allowed to rest at least 3 minutes.

Heat your waffle iron. Spoon the batter onto the hot iron. Cook for 3-4 minutes or until the waffles are done. Every waffle iron cooks differently, so add batter and cook according to your waffle iron directions. Serve with butter and syrup.

Refrigerator Yeast Waffles or Pancakes

This makes thirty six 4" waffles or 36 pancakes. The batter will keep in the refrigerator up to one week. I like to bake all the waffles and freeze them once cooked.

1 pkg. active dry yeast
1/4 cup warm water
4 cups all purpose flour
2 tbs. baking powder
1 tbs. baking soda
1 tsp. salt
2 tbs. granulated sugar
4 cups buttermilk
6 eggs, beaten
1 cup light cream
1/4 cup vegetable oil
2 1/4 cups fresh diced fruit, optional
Butter and syrup

In a small bowl, add the yeast and water. Let the yeast dissolve for 5 minutes. In a large mixing bowl, add the all purpose flour, baking powder, baking soda, salt and granulated sugar. Stir until combined.

Add the buttermilk, eggs, light cream, vegetable oil and yeast mixture. Stir until well blended. Refrigerate the batter until ready to use.

To make waffles, preheat your waffle iron. Spoon the batter and cook according to your waffle maker's directions. Sprinkle 1/4 to 1/2 cup fruit over the waffles if desired. On my waffle iron, it takes about 4 minutes to cook. Cook until the waffles are done and golden brown.

To make pancakes, preheat a griddle or skillet over medium heat. Spray the griddle with non stick cooking spray if desired. Place about 1/4 cup batter per pancake on the griddle. Sprinkle some of the fruit if desired over the pancake. Cook until the top of the pancakes are covered in bubbles. Flip the pancake and cook about 1 minute on the other side. Serve with butter and syrup.

Baked Orange French Toast

Makes 6 servings

1/4 cup granulated sugar
1 tsp. ground cinnamon
6 eggs
1 3/4 cups whole milk
2/3 cup orange marmalade
1/2 tsp. vanilla extract
6 slices bread, cut into 1" cubes
1/3 cup raisins
1 tbs. cornstarch
1/2 tsp. grated orange zest
3/4 cup orange juice
2 tsp. unsalted butter

Preheat the oven to 325°. Spray a 2 quart casserole dish with non stick cooking spray. In a mixing bowl, add the granulated sugar, cinnamon, eggs, milk, 1/3 cup orange marmalade and vanilla extract. Whisk until well combined.

Place the bread cubes in the prepared dish. Sprinkle the raisins over the top of the bread. Pour the egg mixture over the bread cubes and raisins. Using the back of a spatula, lightly press the bread cubes into the egg mixture. All the bread should be coated. Bake for 30-35 minutes.

This casserole is easily over cooked. Cook only until the eggs are set. It may look slightly wet in the center when done. Remove the casserole from the oven and serve with the orange sauce.

Make the sauce while the casserole is cooking. In a small sauce pan over medium low heat, add the cornstarch, orange zest, orange juice and 1/3 cup orange marmalade. Stir constantly and cook until the sauce thickens and bubbles. Remove the sauce from the heat and stir in the butter. Pour the sauce over french toast slices when you are ready to serve.

Caramel Pecan Bubble Ring

Makes 12 servings

1/3 cup chopped pecans
3/4 cup granulated sugar
4 tsp. ground cinnamon
16-20 refrigerated bread sticks (I use Pillsbury refrigerated brand)
1/3 cup unsalted butter, melted
1/2 cup caramel ice cream topping
2 tbs. maple syrup

Preheat the oven to 350°. Spray a 10" tube pan with non stick cooking spray. Spray well or the rolls will stick. Sprinkle half of the pecans in the bottom of the pan. In a small bowl, stir together the granulated sugar and cinnamon.

Separate the bread sticks from the can. Cut each bread stick in half. Dip each bread stick piece in melted butter and then roll the bread stick into the cinnamon sugar. Arrange the bread sticks in the pan forming 2 layers.

Sprinkle the remaining pecans over the bread sticks. In a small bowl, stir together the caramel topping and maple syrup. Drizzle the mixture over the bread sticks. Bake for 25-35 minutes or until the bread is lightly browned. Cover the dish with aluminum foil and cook until the bread is done.

In my oven, it takes about 40 minutes total cooking time. Remove the pan from the oven. Let the bread cool for 1 minute. Invert the pan onto a serving platter. Serve the bread warm. Scrape the pan and remove any pecans and syrup. Drizzle the pan scrapings over the bread. Serve warm.

Apple Cinnamon Rolls

This dough makes a delicious cinnamon roll. Make plenty since they will be gone in a flash. Unbaked rolls can be frozen.

4 1/2 to 5 1/4 cups all purpose flour
1 pkg. active dry yeast
1 cup whole milk
1/3 cup granulated sugar
1/3 cup unsalted butter
1/2 tsp. salt
3 eggs
1 tsp. vegetable oil
1 cup finely chopped apple
Cinnamon Filling recipe below
Vanilla Glaze recipe below

In a large bowl, add 2 1/4 cups all purpose flour and the yeast. Stir until combined. In a sauce pan over low heat, add the milk, granulated sugar, butter and salt. Stir constantly until the granulated sugar dissolves and the butter melts. Do not let the milk boil. You only want to warm the milk. Remove the pan from the heat and cool for 3 minutes.

Add the milk to the flour mixture. Using a mixer on medium speed, beat for 30 seconds. Add the eggs and beat for 1 minute or until well combined. Turn the mixer to high speed and beat for 3 minutes. Turn the mixer off. Using a heavy spoon, stir in as much of the remaining flour as possible. You need a soft dough but the dough should be firm enough to hold together.

Lightly flour your work surface. Turn the dough onto the work surface. Knead about 5 minutes or until the dough is smooth and elastic. Do not add additional flour unless needed to make a smooth dough. Grease a large bowl with the vegetable oil. Place the dough in the bowl and turn the dough to coat the outside of the dough with the oil. Cover the dough and let the dough rise for 1 hour. The dough should be doubled in volume when ready.

Once the dough has risen, remove the dough from the bowl and place on a lightly floured surface. Punch the dough down. Divide the dough into two portions. Cover the dough and let the dough rest for 10 minutes.

Cinnamon Filling: While the dough is resting, make the cinnamon filling. In a mixing bowl, stir together 3/4 cup light brown sugar, 1/4 cup all purpose flour and 1 tablespoon ground cinnamon. Add 1/3 cup chilled unsalted butter. Using a pastry blender, cut the butter into the dry ingredients. The mixture should resemble coarse crumbs. You should still see tiny pieces of the butter when done.

Roll each piece of dough to a 12 x 8 rectangle. Sprinkle the cinnamon filling over each rectangle. Place the apple over each rectangle. Starting with a long side, roll the dough up like a jelly roll. Fold the ends and seal all the edges. Brush the edges lightly with water if needed to seal the edges.

Apple Cinnamon Rolls cont'd

Spray two 9" round cake pans with non stick cooking spray. Using a sharp knife, cut the rolls into 12 slices each. Place the rolls, cut side down, in the cake pans. Cover the dough and let the rolls rise for 30 minutes in a warm place.

Preheat the oven to 375°. Bake the rolls for 20-25 minutes. The rolls should be done and lightly browned. If the rolls are browning too fast, loosely cover them with aluminum foil. Remove the rolls from the oven. Cool the rolls in the pan for 1 minute. Invert the rolls onto a serving plate.

Vanilla Glaze: In a small bowl, stir together 1 1/4 cups powdered sugar, 1 teaspoon light corn syrup and 1/2 teaspoon vanilla extract. Stir in 1 or 2 tablespoons whole milk. The glaze should be thick but thin enough to drizzle on the rolls.

Drizzle the glaze over the hot rolls. Serve the rolls warm.

Chocolate Cinnamon Rolls: Prepare as directed above but substitute 1 cup semi sweet chocolate chips for the apple.

Raisin Pecan Cinnamon Rolls: Prepare as directed above but substitute 1/2 cup chopped pecans and 1/2 cup raisins for the apple.

Orange Bow Knots

Makes 24 rolls

5 1/4 to 5 3/4 cups all purpose flour
1 pkg. active dry yeast
1 1/4 cups whole milk
1/2 cup unsalted butter
1/3 cup granulated sugar
1/2 tsp. salt
2 eggs
2 tbs. grated orange zest
1/4 cup orange juice
1 tsp. vegetable oil
Orange Glaze recipe below

In a large bowl, stir together 2 cups all purpose flour and the yeast. In a sauce pan over low heat, add the milk, butter, granulated sugar and salt. Stir constantly and only heat until the sugar dissolves and the butter melts. Do not let the milk boil. You only want the milk to be lukewarm. Remove the pan from the heat and cool for 3 minutes.

Add the milk to the flour mixture. Using a mixer on medium speed, beat for 30 seconds. Add the eggs and beat for 1 minute or until well combined. Turn the mixer to high speed and beat for 3 minutes. Turn the mixer off. Using a heavy spoon, stir in the orange zest, orange juice and as much of the remaining flour as possible. You need a soft dough but the dough should be firm enough to hold together.

Lightly flour your work surface. Turn the dough onto the work surface. Knead about 5 minutes or until the dough is smooth and elastic. Do not add additional flour unless needed to make a smooth dough. Grease a large bowl with the vegetable oil. Place the dough in the bowl and turn the dough to coat the outside of the dough with the oil. Cover the dough and let the dough rise for 1 hour. The dough should be doubled in volume when ready.

Once the dough has risen, remove the dough from the bowl and place on a lightly floured surface. Punch the dough down. Divide the dough into two portions. Cover the dough and let the dough rest for 10 minutes.

Roll each dough portion into a 12 x 7 rectangle. Cut each rectangle into twelve 7" strips. Tie each strip loosely to form a knot. Spray two baking sheets with non stick cooking spray. Place the rolls on the baking sheet about 2" apart. Cover the rolls and let them rise for 30 minutes. The rolls should be doubled in size. Preheat the oven to 400°. Bake the rolls for 10-12 minutes. The rolls should be done and golden brown. Remove the rolls from the oven and glaze with Orange Glaze. Serve the rolls warm.

Orange Glaze: In a small bowl, stir together 1 cup powdered sugar and 1 teaspoon grated orange zest. Add 1 or 2 tablespoons orange juice. The glaze should be thick but thin enough to drizzle. Drizzle the glaze over the hot rolls.

Cinnamon Muffin Bread

Makes 2 loaves

6 cups all purpose flour
1/2 cup raisins
2 pkgs. active dry yeast
1 tbs. granulated sugar
2 tsp. salt
1 1/2 tsp. ground cinnamon
1/4 tsp. baking soda
2 cups lukewarm whole milk
1/2 cup lukewarm water

In a bowl, combine 3 cups all purpose flour, raisins, yeast, granulated sugar, salt, ground cinnamon and the baking soda. Add the lukewarm milk and water and beat until a dough forms. Stir in enough remaining flour to make a stiff dough. Grease two loaf pans with non stick cooking spray or butter. Divide the dough between the loaf pans and smooth with your hands if needed to form a loaf shape. Let the loaves rise in a warm place for 45 minutes to 1 hour.

Preheat the oven to 400°. Bake the risen loaves in the oven for 25-30 minutes or until done and the top begins to brown. Remove the bread from the pans and cool. Do not slice the bread until it has thoroughly cooled or the crumb will be ruined.

Miniature Lemon Sugar Loaves

Makes 3 miniature loaves

1/2 cup granulated sugar
5 tsp. grated lemon rind
4 tbs. unsalted butter, melted
12 flaky refrigerated biscuits (not Grand's)

Preheat the oven to 375°. In a small bowl, add the granulated sugar and lemon rind. Stir until combined. Place the melted butter in a separate small bowl.

Roll each biscuit in the melted butter and then in the lemon sugar mixture. Place 4 biscuits in each miniature loaf pan. Bake for 15-20 minutes or until the biscuits are done and golden brown.

Chess Squares Coffee Cake

Makes 10 servings

1 1/2 cups unsalted butter, softened
8 oz. softened cream cheese
3 cups granulated sugar
6 eggs
2 tsp. vanilla extract
3 cups all purpose flour
1/4 tsp. salt
1 cup powdered sugar

Preheat the oven to 325°. In a large mixing bowl, beat the cream cheese and the butter until light and fluffy or about 4 minutes. Add the granulated sugar and beat for 3 minutes. Add the eggs, one at a time, beating well after each addition.

Add the vanilla extract, all purpose flour and salt. Mix to combine. Grease a 10" spring form pan or a deep round cake pan. Be sure to grease the pan well or the cake will stick. Pour the batter into the cake pan and bake for one hour and 15 minutes or until the center test done. The center will be firm but will jiggle slightly when done. Cool the cake in the pan for 5 minutes before removing from the pan.

Invert the pan onto a serving plate. Liberally dust the top of the cake with powdered sugar while the cake is still warm.

Blueberry Orange Bread

Makes one loaf

2 tbs. unsalted butter
1/4 cup boiling water
1 tbs. plus 1 tsp. grated orange zest
1/2 cup plus 2 tbs. orange juice
1 egg
1 cup granulated sugar
2 cups all purpose flour
1 tsp. baking powder
1/4 tsp. baking soda
1/2 tsp. salt
1 cup fresh blueberries
2 tbs. honey

Preheat the oven to 350°. Spray a loaf pan with non stick cooking spray. In a small bowl, add the butter and boiling water. Stir until the butter melts. Stir in 1 tablespoon orange zest and 1/2 cup orange juice.

In a separate bowl, add the egg and granulated sugar. Using a mixer on medium speed, beat for 3 minutes. The mixture should be light and fluffy. Add the orange juice mixture and mix only until combined.

Turn the mixer to low. Add the all purpose flour, baking powder, baking soda and salt. Mix only until combined. Turn the mixer off. Gently fold in the blueberries. Spoon the batter into the prepared pan. Bake for 45-55 minutes or until a toothpick inserted in the center of the bread comes out clean.

Remove the bread from the oven and cool the bread in the pan for 10 minutes. Remove the bread from the pan to cool. Make the glaze while the bread is cooling. In a small bowl, add 1 teaspoon orange zest, 2 tablespoons orange juice and the honey. Whisk until well combined. Pour the glaze over the hot bread. Cool the bread completely before slicing.

Easy Sausage Mini Muffins

Makes about 48 mini muffins

3 cups Bisquick
1 lb. ground pork sausage
10 oz. can condensed cheddar cheese soup
1 cup water

In a skillet over medium heat, add the sausage. Stir the sausage frequently to break the meat into crumbles as it cooks. Cook for 7-8 minutes or until the sausage is done and no longer pink. Remove the pan from the heat and drain all the grease from the sausage.

Preheat the oven to 350°. Spray mini muffin tins with non stick cooking spray. Stir the Bisquick, cheese soup and water into the skillet with the sausage. Stir until well combined. Spoon the batter into the prepared muffin cups filling them about 2/3 full. Bake for 10-15 minutes or until the muffins tops are done. Remove the muffins from the oven. Cool the muffins in the pan for 5 minutes. Serve warm.

Buttery Vanilla Breakfast Scones

Makes 16 scones

2 cups all purpose flour
1 tbs. baking powder
4 tbs. granulated sugar
1/2 tsp. salt
4 tbs. chilled unsalted butter, cubed
3/4 cup heavy cream
1 egg, beaten
1 tsp. vanilla extract

Preheat the oven to 400°. In a mixing bowl, add the all purpose flour, baking powder, granulated sugar and salt. Stir until blended. Add the butter and cut the butter into the dry ingredients with a pastry blender. The mixture should resemble coarse crumbs. You should still be able to see tiny pieces of butter when done.

Stir in the heavy cream, egg and vanilla extract. Stir only until blended. Do not over mix. I use my hands to combine the ingredients. Lightly flour your work surface. Place the dough on the surface. Divide the dough into 4 pieces. Shape each piece into a round disk. Place each disk on a parchment lined baking pan.

Cut each disk into 4 wedges and separate the wedges. Bake for 12-15 minutes. The bottoms will be golden brown and the scones flaky tender when done. Remove the scones from the oven and serve with your favorite jam.

Blackberry Dumplings

Makes 8 servings

1 pie crust dough recipe for a double crust pie
2 cups fresh or thawed frozen blackberries
1 cup water
1 cup granulated sugar
1 stick unsalted butter

Preheat the oven to 350°. Roll the pie crust dough into a large rectangle. Cut the dough into eight 4" squares. Place about 1/4 cup of the blackberries in the center of each dough square. To make the dumplings, fold up the corners of the dough squares and pinch the edges together with the seams on top of the blackberries.

Place the dumplings in a baking dish and prick each dumpling several times with a fork. In a saucepan over medium heat, add the granulated sugar, butter and the water. Cook until the butter melts and the granulated sugar is dissolved. Pour the sauce over the dumplings. Bake for 30-40 minutes or until the dumplings are golden brown. Remove the dumplings from the oven and cool for 5 minutes before serving.

Puff Pancake with Summer Berries

Makes 6 servings

2 cups blueberries
1 cup sliced strawberries
1 cup raspberries
Granulated sugar to taste
4 tbs. unsalted butter,melted
2 eggs
1/2 cup all purpose flour
1/2 cup whole milk
1 tbs. granulated sugar
1/4 tsp. salt

In a large bowl, add the blueberries, strawberries and raspberries. Sprinkle granulated sugar over the berries to taste. Gently stir to combine the berries with the sugar. Let the berries sit at room temperature until ready to use.

Preheat the oven to 425°. In an oven proof skillet, add 2 tablespoons butter. Place the skillet in the oven for 3 minutes. The butter should be bubbly. Remove the pan from the oven and tilt the pan to coat the bottom and sides of the skillet with butter.

In a mixing bowl, add the eggs and 2 tablespoons butter. Using a mixer on high speed, beat for 3 minutes. Reduce the mixer speed to medium and add the all purpose flour, milk, granulated sugar and salt. Mix only until combined. Pour the batter into the hot skillet. Bake for 15 minutes. Reduce the heat to 350°. Bake for 10-12 minutes or until the pancake puffs. Remove the pancake from the oven and spoon the berries over the pancake. Serve immediately.

Blueberry Peach Breakfast Pudding

Makes 6 servings

2 cups fresh blueberries
2 cups fresh sliced peaches
1 1/2 cups granulated sugar
3 tbs. softened unsalted butter
1/2 cup whole milk
1 tsp. baking powder
1 tsp. salt
1 cup all purpose flour
1 tbs. cornstarch
1 cup boiling water

Preheat the oven to 300°. Grease a 9" square pan with nonstick cooking spray. Arrange the blueberries and the peaches in the bottom of the pan. In a mixing bowl, add 1/2 cup granulated sugar and the butter. Beat with an electric mixer until light and fluffy or about 2 minutes. Add the whole milk, baking powder, salt and all purpose flour. Beat until well combined. Pour the dough over the fruit.

In a measuring cup, add the cornstarch and 1 cup granulated sugar. Sprinkle the mixture over the dough. Pour the boiling water over the dough. Do not stir the batter. Bake for 30-45 minutes or until set. Serve warm or cold.

Seafood Rice Salad

Makes 6 servings

8 oz. cooked shrimp
3 cups cooked rice, cooled
1/2 cup finely chopped sweet pickles
1/4 cup diced pimentos
1 tbs. fresh lemon juice
7 oz. can tuna, drained
1/2 cup finely chopped onion
1 cup thinly sliced celery
3 hard boiled eggs, chopped
1 cup mayonnaise
12 tomato wedges

Combine all the ingredients, except the tomatoes, in a serving bowl. Toss to mix the ingredients. Chill at least 2 hours before serving.

To serve, place 2 tomato wedges on a serving dish. Scoop the rice salad on top of the tomato wedges.

Puffed Salad Bowl with Ham Salad

Makes 4 servings

2/3 cup water
1/4 cup unsalted butter
1 cup Bisquick
4 eggs
10 oz. pkg. frozen green peas, thawed
2 cups smoked ham, diced
2 tbs. chopped onion
1 cup shredded cheddar cheese
3/4 cup mayonnaise
1 1/2 tsp. yellow prepared mustard

The first step is to make the ham salad. In a large bowl, add the frozen green peas, ham, onion, cheddar cheese, mayonnaise and the mustard. Stir until well combined. Refrigerate at least 2 hours or overnight if desired.

Preheat the oven to 400°. To make the salad bowl puff, mix together the water and butter in a small sauce pan over medium heat. Stir constantly while making the salad bowl puff. When the butter is melted and the water is boiling, pour in the Bisquick. Stir vigorously until the dough forms into a ball. This will take about 2 minutes. Remove the pan from the heat. Beat in the eggs, one at a time, until well combined. The batter should be smooth.

Spray a 9" pie plate with non stick cooking spray. Pour the batter into the pie pan. Do not try to spoon the batter up the sides of the pie plate. It will "puff" on its own during baking. Bake for 35-40 minutes or until the center is puffed and dry. Remove the salad bowl from the oven.

Spoon the ham salad into the pie plate. Cut into wedges and serve.

Try the salad puff with chicken salad, roast beef or any ingredients you desire. It is good with scrambled eggs and bacon in the center of the crust. I also like it with fresh fruit and whipped cream.

Rotel Grits

Makes 6 servings

2 cups water
1 3/4 cups whole milk or half & half
1 tsp. salt
1 cup quick cooking grits
1/2 cup unsalted butter
10 oz. can Rotel tomatoes
8 oz. Velveeta cheese, cubed or shredded

In a large sauce pan, add the water, salt and 1 1/4 cups milk. Bring the liquids to a boil over medium heat. Add the grits and Rotel tomatoes including the juice. Stir constantly and bring to a boil. Boil for 1 minute.

Reduce the heat to low and cover the pan with a lid. Simmer for 8-10 minutes or until the grits are thick and creamy. Depending upon the brand of grits used, you may need to add the remaining milk.

Remove the pan from the heat and stir in the butter until melted. Add the cheese and stir until melted. Let the grits sit for a few minutes before serving. The grits will firm up as they cool.

Pear Macaroon Salad

Pears, cream cheese and macaroons. What's not to love? Makes 4 servings.

8 canned pear halves
8 oz. pkg. cream cheese, softened
2 tbs. mayonnaise
1 1/2 cups crushed macaroon cookies
4 maraschino cherries

Drain the pears reserving the juice. In a mixing bowl, add the reserved pear juice, cream cheese and mayonnaise. Whisk until well combined.

Place the pear halves on a serving platter. Fill each pear half with the cream cheese mixture. Press two pear halves together. Roll the pears in the macaroon crumbs. Coat the pears thoroughly with the cookie crumbs.

Sit the pear upright on a serving plate and top each pear with a maraschino cherry. The cherry replaces the pear stem.

Note: You can replace the macaroon cookies with sugar cookies, vanilla wafers, graham crackers or any hard cookie you desire.

Honey Fruit Salad

Makes 6 servings

15 oz. can pineapple chunks
2 oranges, peeled and sectioned
1 apple, peeled and diced
1 banana, peeled and sliced
1/2 cup chopped pecans
1/2 cup orange juice
1 tbs. fresh lemon juice
1/4 cup honey

In a small bowl, stir together the orange juice, lemon juice and honey. In a serving bowl, add the pineapple chunks including the juice, oranges, apple, banana and pecans. Pour the honey mixture over the fruit. Toss to coat the fruit. Chill at least 1 hour before serving.

Sweetened Grapes

Makes 12 servings

1 lb. green seedless grapes
1 lb. red seedless grapes
1/2 cup sour cream
4 oz. cream cheese, softened
1/2 cup granulated sugar
1/2 cup light brown sugar
1/2 cup chopped pecans

Rinse the grapes. Dry the grapes thoroughly. If the grapes are not dry, the sauce will not stick to them.

In a serving bowl, add the sour cream, cream cheese and granulated sugar. Mix until well combined. Add the grapes and toss to combine. Sprinkle the brown sugar and pecans over the top. Refrigerate until ready to serve.

Banana Split Salad

Makes 8 servings

14 oz. can sweetened condensed milk
12 oz. container Cool Whip
21 oz. can cherry pie filling
3 bananas, sliced
8 oz. can crushed pineapple, drained
1/2 cup chopped pecans
1/2 cup flaked sweetened coconut
1 cup sliced fresh strawberries

In a serving bowl, combine all the ingredients. Chill at least 2 hours before serving.

Cherry Pineapple Cups

Makes 6 servings

4 serving size pkg. cherry jello
1 cup boiling water
1 cup ice water
2 1/2 cups diced fresh pineapple

In a mixing bowl, combine the jello with the boiling water. Stir until the jello is completely dissolved. This usually takes a minute or two. Stir in the ice water. Pour the jello into an 9" square pan. Chill until firm.

When the jello is firm, cut the jello into cubes. Place the pineapple and jello cubes into sherbet glasses and chill until ready to serve.

Cinnamon Honey Butter

Serve this butter over pancakes, waffles and biscuits.

Makes 1/2 cup butter

1/2 cup unsalted butter, softened
1/4 cup powdered sugar
1/4 cup honey
1/2 tsp. ground cinnamon

Place all the ingredients in a mixing bowl. Stir until well combined and fluffy. Spoon into a small serving bowl. Chill until firm.

9 BEVERAGES

Beverages make a party. I have included alcoholic and non alcoholic drinks. If you serve alcohol at your party, be sure to follow safe driving rules. Do not let you or your guest drink and drive.

Whether you need a punch or just a simple beverage for brunch, recipes are included for all occasions.

Champagne Peach Punch

Makes 12 servings

16 oz. pkg. frozen unsweetened peach slices
1/4 cup granulated sugar
2 1/2 cups orange juice
2 tbs. lemon juice
750 ml bottle champagne
Cubed or crushed ice

Thaw the peaches at room temperature. Place the peaches with any juice and the granulated sugar in a blender. Blend until smooth. Pour the peaches into a 2 quart pitcher. Stir in the orange juice and lemon juice. Refrigerate until ready to serve.

When you are ready to serve, add the champagne to the pitcher. Gently tilt the champagne bottle up and down when pouring to create bubbles. Serve over ice.

Orange Mint Juleps

Makes 8 servings

2 cups water
2/3 cup granulated sugar
1 cup fresh mint
1 tsp. grated orange zest
2 cups orange juice
2/3 cup lemon juice
1/3 cup bourbon
Ice cubes

In a sauce pan over medium heat, add the water and granulated sugar. Bring the mixture to a boil. Stir constantly until the sugar dissolves. Place the mint in a heat proof bowl. Pour the water mixture over the mint. Stir in the orange zest, orange juice and lemon juice.

Let the julep sit at room temperature for 1 hour. Pour the mixture through a strainer. Pour the julep mixture into a pitcher and add the bourbon. Stir until combined. Serve in tall stemmed glasses over ice.

Trader's Punch

Makes 1 gallon

2 cups orange juice
2 cups lemon juice
1 cup grenadine syrup
1/2 cup light corn syrup
3 liters ginger ale, chilled

In a one gallon pitcher, add the orange juice, lemon juice, grenadine syrup and corn syrup. Stir until well combined. Chill until ready to use. When ready to serve, add the ginger ale.

Serve over ice cubes or in a punch bowl.

Cranberry Punch

Makes 16 punch cup servings

2/3 cup granulated sugar
3 cinnamon sticks
2 tsp. whole allspice
1 tsp. whole cloves
1/4 tsp. salt
4 cups cranberry juice cocktail
2 1/2 cups unsweetened pineapple juice
3 1/2 cups chilled ginger ale
6 orange slices
3 cups ice cubes

In a sauce pan over medium heat, add the granulated sugar, cinnamon sticks, allspice, cloves, salt, pineapple juice and cranberry juice cocktail. Set the pan over low heat and simmer for 10 minutes. Remove the pan from the heat and strain. Place the punch in a pitcher and refrigerate until well chilled.

When ready to serve, add the ice cubes to a punch bowl. Pour the ginger ale into the punch bowl. Add the punch mixture and stir until combined. Float orange slices over the top of the punch.

Tea Berry Sangria

Makes 2 quarts

2 cups water
3/4 cup granulated sugar
1 orange, sliced
1 lemon, sliced
1 lime, sliced
4 regular size tea bags
2 cups red wine
10 oz. pkg. frozen sliced strawberries, thawed
2 cups Sprite

In a sauce pan over medium heat, add the water and granulated sugar. Bring the mixture to a boil and add the orange, lemon and lime slices. Boil for 1 minute. Remove the pan from the heat and add the tea bags. Cover the pan with a lid and let the tea steep for 5 minutes. Remove the tea bags and pour the mixture into a 2 quart pitcher. Refrigerate until well chilled.

When ready to serve, puree the strawberries in a blender. Add the strawberries, wine and Sprite to the pitcher. Stir until combined and serve over ice.

Red Roosters

Makes 3 quarts

32 oz. bottle cranberry juice cocktail
12 oz. can frozen orange juice concentrate, thawed
4 1/2 cups water
2 cups vodka

Combine all the ingredients in a large mixing bowl. Place the bowl in the freezer until frozen.

When ready to serve, remove the mixture from the freezer and spoon into a blender. Process until the drink reaches the consistency you desire. Serve at once.

Whiskey Sour Punch

Makes 18 servings

6 oz. can frozen orange juice concentrate
6 oz. can frozen lemon juice concentrate
1 tbs. angostura bitters
2 tbs. granulated sugar
8 oz. jar maraschino cherries
3/4 quart whiskey sour cocktail, chilled
1 liter bottle club soda, chilled
8 cups ice cubes
1 navel orange, thinly sliced
1 lemon, thinly sliced

Drain the maraschino cherries but save the juice. In a large pitcher, add the orange juice concentrate, lemon juice concentrate, bitters, granulated sugar and maraschino cherry juice. Let the juices thaw at room temperature. When the juices thaw, stir in the maraschino cherries. Stir until combined. Refrigerate at least 4 hours.

When ready to serve, place the juice mixture, whiskey sour cocktail and club soda in a punch bowl. Add the ice cubes and stir to combine. Place the orange and lemon slices on the top of the punch.

Daiquiri Punch Bowl

Makes 16 servings

24 ice cubes
16 oz. bottle daiquiri mix
6 tbs. powdered sugar
2 1/2 cups light rum
1/2 cup orange flavored liqueur
1 liter bottle club soda, chilled

In a pitcher, add the daiquiri mix and powdered sugar. Stir until the sugar dissolves. Stir in the rum and orange liqueur. Refrigerate for 4 hours. Stir occasionally to keep the punch mixed.

When ready to serve, add half the punch and 12 ice cubes to a blender. Puree until the ice cubes are crushed. Pour into a large pitcher. Repeat with the remaining punch and ice cubes. Stir in the club soda and serve.

Orange Blossoms

Makes 16 servings

3 cups orange juice
1/2 cup lemon juice
1/2 cup grenadine juice
3/4 quart martini cocktail, chilled
1 liter club soda, chilled

In a large pitcher, add the orange juice, lemon juice and grenadine juice. Stir until combined. Refrigerate for 4 hours.

When ready to serve, add the juice to a punch bowl. Stir in the martini cocktail and club soda.

Orange and Strawberry Cream

Makes 2 servings

1/2 cup plain yogurt
3/4 cup strawberry yogurt
3/4 cup orange juice
1 1/4 cups frozen strawberries
1 banana, sliced and frozen

Place all the ingredients in a blender and process until smooth.

Blueberry Apple Juice Blast

Makes 2 servings

3/4 cup chilled apple juice
1/2 cup plain yogurt
1 banana, sliced and frozen
1 cup frozen blueberries

Place all the ingredients in a blender. Process until smooth.

Melon Mango Juice

Makes 4 servings

1 cantaloupe, peeled and diced
2 1/2 cups mango juice
2 tbs. orange juice

Place all the ingredients in a blender. Process until smooth.

Louisiana Cherry Bounce

Makes 2 quarts

This is an old recipe and it takes 2 weeks to make. Your guest will love it!

2 quarts wild cherries, stemmed and cleaned
3 cups granulated sugar
1 quart bourbon

In a gallon glass bowl, add the cherries and granulated sugar. Stir until combined. Cover the bowl with cloth. Do not put a lid on the bowl. Place the bowl in a cool spot for 2 weeks. Stir the cherries every other day.

After 2 weeks, stir in the bourbon. Let the mixture sit for 24 hours. Strain the mixture through cheese cloth. Serve over ice.

10 LEFTOVERS

We all have leftovers after the holidays. We never want to throw the food away so looking for leftover recipes can be trying. I have included my families favorite leftover recipes.

With just a little preparation, you can turn leftovers into a new meal. Your family will love them and appreciate not having to eat the same food for days. These leftover recipes aren't just for the holidays. Use them for leftovers all year round.

Savory Turkey Pecan Waffles

This is my families favorite way to eat leftover turkey.

Makes 4 servings

Waffles

1 3/4 cups all purpose flour
3 tsp. baking powder
1/2 tsp. salt
2 egg yolks, beaten
1 3/4 cups whole milk
1/2 cup vegetable oil
2 egg whites, beaten to stiff peaks

Turkey Pecan Sauce

1/4 cup unsalted butter
3 chicken bouillon cubes
1/3 cup all purpose flour
1/4 tsp. poultry seasoning
2 1/2 cups whole milk
1 tbs. lemon juice
2 cups cooked cubed turkey
1/2 cup chopped celery
1/2 cup chopped pecans
2 tbs. chopped red pimento

To make the waffles, preheat your waffle iron. In a mixing bowl, add the all purpose flour, baking powder and salt. Stir until combined. In a separate bowl, add the egg yolks, milk and vegetable oil. Whisk until well blended. Add to the dry ingredients. Mix only until combined. Gently fold in the beaten egg whites.

Spray your waffle iron with non stick cooking spray if desired. Spoon the batter onto your waffle iron following your waffle iron maker's directions for the amount of batter. Cook for 4-5 minutes or until the waffles are done and golden brown. Cook the waffles according to your waffle maker's directions. Keep the waffles warm.

While the waffles are baking, prepare the sauce. In a sauce pan over medium heat, add the butter and bouillon cubes. Crush the bouillon cubes with the back of a spoon. Stir in the all purpose flour and poultry seasoning. Stir constantly while making the sauce. Add the milk and lemon juice. Cook until the sauce thickens and bubbles. Add the turkey, celery, 2 tablespoons pecans and red pimento. Cook only until the turkey and celery are hot. Remove the sauce from the pan and serve over the waffles.

Sprinkle the remaining pecans over the waffles when serving.

Turkey Cheese Bake

Makes 4 servings

10.75 oz. can cream of chicken soup
8 oz. jar processed cheese spread
1/2 cup whole milk
2 cups leftover cooked turkey, diced
3 tbs. canned green chiles, diced
2 tsp. dried minced onion
4 cups corn chips

Preheat the oven to 350°. Spray a 2 quart casserole dish with non stick cooking spray. In a sauce pan over medium low heat, add the cream of chicken soup and cheese spread. Stir until heated through. Stir in the milk, turkey, green chiles and onion. Stir frequently and cook until the mixture bubbles. Remove the pan from the heat.

Crush half of the corn chips and place them in the bottom of the casserole dish. Spoon the filling over the corn chips. Sprinkle the remaining corn chips over the top. Bake for 20 minutes. The casserole should be hot and bubbly. Remove the casserole from the oven and cool for 5 minutes before serving.

Turkey Chowder

Makes 8 servings

4 slices bacon, diced
1 cup chopped onion
4 cups potato, peeled and cubed
2 cups chicken broth or turkey broth
2 pkgs. 10 oz. size frozen whole kernel corn
1/4 cup unsalted butter
2 1/2 tsp. salt
1/4 tsp. black pepper
2 cups leftover cooked turkey, cubed
2 cups whole milk
1 cup heavy cream
2 tbs. minced fresh parsley
Oyster crackers

In a dutch oven, add the bacon. Place the pan over medium heat and cook for 4-5 minutes or until the bacon is done and crisp. Remove the bacon from the pot and drain on paper towels.

Add the onion to the pot and saute the onion for 5 minutes. Add the potatoes and chicken broth. Bring the soup to a boil. Place a lid on the pot and reduce the heat to low. Simmer for 30 minutes. The potato should be tender but not mushy.

In a separate sauce pan over medium heat, add the corn, butter, salt, black pepper, turkey and milk. Stir occasionally and simmer for 5 minutes. The corn should be tender. Add the mixture to the pot with the potatoes. Stir in the heavy cream. Cook only until the cream is heated through. Do not let the chowder boil. Remove the soup from the pot. Ladle the soup into bowls and sprinkle each bowl with parsley and bacon. Serve with oyster crackers.

Turkey Hawaiian

Makes 6 servings

1 cup chopped onion
2 tbs. vegetable oil
10 oz. pkg. frozen green peas
1 1/2 cups sliced celery
2 chicken bouillon cubes
3/4 cup water
2 tbs. cornstarch
1 tbs. soy sauce
14 oz. can pineapple tidbits
4 oz. can sliced mushrooms
5 oz. can sliced water chestnuts, drained
3 cups cooked turkey, cut into julienne strips
3 cups cooked rice

In a skillet over medium heat, add the onion and vegetable oil. Saute the onion for 4 minutes. Stir in the green peas, celery, bouillon cubes and water. Place a lid on the pan. Bring the mixture to a boil and cook for 5 minutes.

Stir to combine the ingredients with the liquid. In a small bowl, stir together the cornstarch and soy sauce. Add to the skillet along with the pineapples with juice, mushrooms with liquid and water chestnuts. Stir until well combined. Cook until the sauce thickens and boils. Add the cooked turkey and cook only until the turkey is warmed.

Place the rice on a serving platter. Spoon the turkey mixture over the rice to serve.

Turkey Stroganoff

My family loves this classic anytime of the year. I love it uses leftover turkey and leftover gravy. Substitute jarred gravy if desired.

Makes 4 servings

1 cup chopped onion
2 tbs. unsalted butter
3 cups cooked turkey, cut into thin strips
1 1/2 cups turkey gravy
2 tbs. ketchup
1 cup sour cream
2 cups hot cooked egg noodles
2 tbs. fresh minced parsley

In a skillet over medium heat, add the onion and butter. Saute the onion for 5 minutes. Add the turkey, gravy and ketchup. Stir constantly and simmer for 5 minutes. Stir in the sour cream and cook for 1minute. Remove the skillet from the heat and fold in the hot cooked noodles. Spoon the stroganoff onto a serving platter. Sprinkle the parsley over the top.

Turkey & Ham Rice Skillet

Makes 6 servings

1/2 cup chopped onion
1 garlic clove, minced
2 tbs. unsalted butter
1 tsp. salt
1/2 tsp. chili powder
1/8 tsp. cayenne pepper
1 bay leaf
32 oz. can diced tomatoes
2 cups cooked diced turkey
2 cups diced cooked ham
1 cup uncooked rice
1 tbs. minced fresh parsley

In a large skillet over medium heat, add the onion, garlic and butter. Saute the onion and garlic for 4 minutes. Stir in the salt, chili powder, cayenne pepper, bay leaf, diced tomatoes with juice, turkey, ham, rice and parsley. Place a lid on the skillet and bring to a boil. Reduce the heat to low. Simmer for 30-40 minutes or until the rice is tender. Remove the bay leaf and serve.

Turkey Salad Bake

Makes 4 servings

2 cups finely crushed potato chips
1/2 cup shredded sharp cheddar cheese
1/2 cup chopped walnuts
1 tbs. unsalted butter
2 cups cubed cooked turkey
2 cups thinly sliced celery
2 tsp. grated onion
1/4 tsp. salt
2 tbs. lemon juice
1/2 cup mayonnaise

In a mixing bowl, add the potato chips and cheddar cheese. Stir until combined. Press half of the potato chip mixture into the bottom of a 2 quart casserole dish.

Preheat the oven to 450°. In a skillet over medium heat, add the walnuts and butter. Saute the walnuts about 15 minutes or until the walnuts are toasted. Remove the skillet from the heat. Stir in the turkey, celery, onion, salt, lemon juice and mayonnaise. Spoon the mixture into the casserole dish. Sprinkle the remaining potato chip mixture over the top.

Bake for 15 minutes or until the casserole is hot and golden brown.

Savory Turkey Scallop

Makes 12 servings

4 cups diced cooked turkey
3 cups soft fine bread crumbs
1 1/2 cups cooked rice
3/4 cup chopped onion
3/4 cup chopped celery
1/3 cup chopped red pimento
3/4 tsp. salt
3/4 tsp. poultry seasoning
1 1/2 cups chicken broth
1 1/2 cups whole milk
4 eggs, beaten
Mushroom Sauce, optional

If you have rice leftover from a casserole, use that instead of cooked rice. I use leftover broccoli rice casserole when I have it.

Preheat the oven to 350°. Spray a 9 x 13 baking dish with non stick cooking spray. Add all the ingredients to the dish. Stir until combined. Bake for 40-50 minutes or until the casserole is hot and bubbly. The top should be lightly browned. Remove the casserole from the oven and serve.

You can serve leftover turkey gravy over the dish if desired. If you want to make an easy sauce, make the Mushroom Sauce.

In a sauce pan over low heat, add 1/4 cup whole milk, 10.75 oz. can cream of mushroom soup and 1 cup sour cream. Stir constantly and heat only until the sauce is hot. Do not let the sauce boil. Serve over the casserole. This sauce is also delicious over potatoes, rice, biscuits and most any meat.

Swiss Turkey Ham Bake

Makes 6 servings

1/2 cup chopped onion
5 tbs. unsalted butter, melted
3 tbs. all purpose flour
1/2 tsp. salt
1/4 tsp. black pepper
3 oz. can sliced mushrooms
1 cup light cream
2 tbs. dry sherry
2 cups leftover cooked turkey, cubed
1 cup cooked ham, cubed
5 oz. can sliced water chestnuts
1/2 cup shredded Swiss cheese
1 1/2 cups soft bread crumbs

In a sauce pan over medium heat, add the onion and 2 tablespoons butter. Saute the onion for 4 minutes. Stir in the all purpose flour. Cook for 1 minute. Add the salt, black pepper, mushrooms with liquid, cream and sherry. Stir constantly and cook until the sauce thickens and bubbles. Stir in the turkey, ham and water chestnuts.

Preheat the oven to 400°. Spoon the mixture into a 2 quart casserole dish. Sprinkle the Swiss cheese over the top. Sprinkle the bread crumbs over the top. Drizzle 3 tablespoons melted butter over the bread crumbs. Remove the casserole from the heat and cool for 5 minutes before serving.

Ham Turkey Noodle Casserole

Makes 6 servings

1/4 cup unsalted butter
1/4 cup all purpose flour
1/2 tsp. salt
1 cup whole milk
1 cup light cream
1/2 cup cooked sliced mushrooms
2 tsp. dried minced onion
2 tsp. yellow prepared mustard
1 cup sour cream
1 1/2 cups cooked ham, cubed
1 1/2 cups cooked turkey, cubed
2 tbs. slivered toasted almonds

In a sauce pan over medium heat, add the butter. When the butter melts, stir in the all purpose flour and salt. Cook for 1 minute or just until the flour begins to brown. Stir constantly while making the sauce. Add the milk, light cream, mushrooms, onion and mustard. Cook until the sauce thickens and bubbles. Remove the pan from the heat and stir in the sour cream, turkey and ham.

Preheat the oven to 325°. Spoon the mixture into a 2 quart casserole dish. Sprinkle the almonds over the top. Bake for 20-30 minutes. The casserole should be hot and bubbly. The almonds should be golden.

Ham and Cheese Casserole

Makes 8 servings

8 oz. dried seashell macaroni
2 cups sliced fresh mushrooms
1/4 cup chopped onion
1/4 cup unsalted butter, melted
1/4 cup all purpose flour
2 cups chicken broth
1 1/4 cups light cream
1 cup shredded cheddar cheese
1 tsp. lemon juice
1/8 tsp. black pepper
3 cups diced cooked ham
1/4 cup grated Parmesan cheese

In a sauce pan over medium heat, add 2 quarts water. Bring the water to a boil. When the water boils, add the macaroni. Cook for 6-8 minutes or until the macaroni is tender. Remove the pan from the heat and drain the water from the macaroni.

In a skillet over medium heat, add the mushrooms, onion and butter. Saute the mushrooms and onion for 5 minutes. Stir constantly and add the all purpose flour. The mixture should be smooth and well blended. Keep stirring and add the chicken broth and light cream. Cook until the sauce thickens and bubbles.

Reduce the heat to low and stir in the cheddar cheese, lemon juice and black pepper. Stir frequently and simmer for 10 minutes. Preheat the oven to 350°. Spray a 3 quart baking dish with non stick cooking spray.

Add the macaroni, ham and sauce from skillet to the baking dish. Stir until well combined. Sprinkle the Parmesan cheese over the top. Bake for 20-30 minutes. The dish should be hot and bubbly when ready.

Alabama Ham Bake

Makes 6 servings

2 sweet potatoes, peeled and thinly sliced
3 pears, peeled, cored and sliced
3 cups diced cooked ham
3 tbs. light brown sugar
1/2 tsp. salt
1/4 tsp. black pepper
1/4 tsp. curry powder
1/3 cup apple cider
1 cup pancake mix
1/2 tsp. dry mustard
1 cup whole milk
2 tbs. unsalted butter, melted

Preheat the oven to 375°. Spray a 2 quart rectangular casserole dish with non stick cooking spray. Lay half of the sweet potatoes in the bottom of the dish. Place half of the pear slices over the sweet potatoes. Sprinkle 1 1/2 cups ham over the pears.

In a small bowl, add the brown sugar, salt, black pepper and curry powder. Stir until well blended. Sprinkle half the seasonings over the ingredients in the dish. Repeat the layering process one more time using the remaining sweet potatoes, pears, ham and seasonings. Pour the apple cider over the top of the dish. Place a lid on the casserole or cover with aluminum foil.

Bake for 40 minutes or until the sweet potatoes are tender. While the casserole is cooking, mix together the pancake mix, dry mustard, milk and melted butter. Remove the lid or aluminum foil. When the sweet potatoes are done, pour the pancake mix over the top of the casserole. Bake for 20 minutes or until the pancake batter is puffed and golden brown. Remove the dish from the oven and serve.

Ham & Cheese Delight

Makes 6 servings

1/2 cup finely chopped onion
1 tbs. unsalted butter
2 cups finely chopped ham
3 beaten eggs
1 cup shredded sharp cheddar cheese
2/3 cup finely crushed crackers
1 1/2 cups whole milk
1/8 tsp. black pepper

Preheat the oven to 350°. Spray a 2 quart casserole dish with non stick cooking spray. In a sauce pan over medium heat, add the butter and onion. Saute the onion for 4 minutes. Stir in the ham, eggs, cheddar cheese, crackers, milk and black pepper. Remove the pan from the heat.

Spoon the mixture into the casserole dish. Bake for 40-50 minutes or until a knife inserted in the center of the casserole comes out clean. Remove the dish from the oven and cool for 5 minutes before serving.

Ham and Apple Scallop

Makes 6 servings

3 cups diced ham
4 tart apples, peeled, cored and sliced
1/4 cup light brown sugar
1/4 tsp. ground mace
1/4 tsp. black pepper
1/4 cup apple juice
1 cup pancake mix
1 cup whole milk
2 tbs. unsalted butter, melted

Preheat the oven to 350°. Spray a 2 quart casserole dish with non stick cooking spray. Layer half of the ham and apples in the casserole dish. In a small bowl, add the brown sugar, mace and black pepper. Stir to combine the seasonings. Sprinkle half the seasonings over the ham and apple. Place the remaining ham and apple in the casserole dish. Sprinkle the remaining seasoning over the top. Pour the apple juice over the top of the dish. Cover the dish with a lid or aluminum foil. Bake for 30-40 minutes or until the apples are tender.

While the dish is baking, make the pancake batter. In a mixing bowl, stir together the pancake mix, milk and melted butter. Remove the lid or aluminum foil from the dish. When the apples are tender, pour the pancake batter over the top. Bake for 15-20 minutes or until the pancake is puffed and golden brown.

Remove the dish from the oven and serve.

Ham Puffs with Mushroom Sauce

Makes 6 servings

1 1/2 cups ground cooked ham
1 cup shredded American cheese
1/4 cup finely chopped green bell pepper
1/4 cup finely chopped onion
2 1/4 cups whole milk
2 egg yolks, beaten
2 cups soft bread crumbs
2 egg whites, beaten to stiff peaks
3 tbs. unsalted butter
3 tbs. all purpose flour
3 oz. can sliced mushrooms
1 tbs. grated onion
1 tbs. fresh minced parsley
1/4 tsp. salt
1/8 tsp. black pepper

Spray six 6 ounce custard cups with non stick cooking spray. Place the cups in a roasting pan. In a mixing bowl, add the ham, American cheese, green bell pepper, onion, 1 1/4 cups milk, egg yolks and bread crumbs. Stir until well combined. Fold in the egg whites. Spoon the mixture into the custard cups.

Pour hot water up to 1" around the custard cups. Bake for 35-45 minutes. The ham puffs should be set. Remove the pan from the oven and place the custard cups on serving plates.

Make the mushroom sauce about 10 minutes before the ham puffs are ready. In a sauce pan over medium heat, add the butter. When the butter melts, stir in the all purpose flour. Stir constantly while making the sauce. Cook the flour for 1 minute. Add the mushrooms with any liquid and 1 cup milk. Cook until the sauce thickens and bubbles. Add the onion, parsley, salt and black pepper. Remove the pan from the heat and serve the sauce over the ham puffs.

Cheesy Ham Sandwiches

Makes 4 sandwiches

8 slices bread (use your favorite brand)
2 tbs. softened unsalted butter
2 cups ground cooked ham
1/2 cup shredded American cheese
2 tbs. finely chopped onion
1/2 tsp. prepared horseradish
4 lettuce leaves
4 thick tomato slices

Preheat the oven to 350°. Spread the bread on one side with the softened butter. Place the butter side down on a baking sheet. Place the bread in the oven and cook until toasted. Remove the bread from the oven.

In a mixing bowl, add the ground ham, cheese, onion and horseradish. Stir until combined. Spread the ham on 4 toasted bread slices. Top each sandwich with a lettuce leaf and tomato slice. Top with the remaining bread slice and serve.

Place leftover ham in a food processor to grind. Easy and simple way to use up leftover ham.

Ham and Fresh Pear Sandwiches

Makes 6 servings

1 loaf French bread, halved lengthwise
1/4 cup unsalted butter, softened
3 oz. cream cheese, softened
1 tbs. whole milk
2 tbs. honey
1 tbs. mayonnaise
1 large ripe pear, thinly sliced
4 Bibb lettuce leaves
1 tsp. lemon juice
6 slices leftover ham

Preheat the oven to 350°. Spread the cut side of the bread with butter. Place the bread on a baking sheet and cook only until toasted. Remove the bread from the oven.

In a small bowl, add the cream cheese, milk and mayonnaise. Stir until combined. Spread the cream cheese over one portion of the bread. Drizzle the honey over the cream cheese. Place lettuce leaves on the sandwich. Place the pear slices over the lettuce. Sprinkle the lemon juice over the pear. Place the ham slices on the sandwich. Place the remaining bread over the top. Cut into 6 pieces and serve.

Fruit Crowned Ham Steak

Makes 4 servings

4 thick cooked ham slices
16 oz. can peach halves
4 slices canned pineapple
1 tbs. yellow prepared mustard

Preheat the oven to 350°. Trim all the fat from the ham if needed. Drain the peaches but reserve the syrup in a small bowl. Add the mustard to the peach syrup and stir until combined.

Brush the peach syrup mixture over the ham slices. Place the ham slices in a shallow baking dish. Lay one pineapple slice over each ham slice. Place the peach halves over the ham and pineapple.

Bake for 45 minutes. Baste the ham and fruit every 15 minutes with the pan juices. Remove the ham from the oven and cool for 10 minutes before serving.

Ham Shortcakes

This is a wonderful after Easter leftover recipe. It uses up leftover ham and hard boiled eggs.

Makes 6 servings

3 cups Bisquick
1/2 cup sliced green onions
4 1/2 cups whole milk
8 tbs. unsalted butter
2 cups diced cooked ham
6 tbs. all purpose flour
1/4 tsp. black pepper
1 tsp. Worcestershire sauce
1 chicken bouillon cube
6 hard boiled eggs, peeled and diced
2 tbs. minced fresh parsley

Preheat the oven to 450°. In a mixing bowl, add the Bisquick, green onions and 1 cup whole milk. Stir until the dough forms. On a baking sheet, drop half of the dough into 6 equal sized portions. Spread the dough out on the baking pan to make 3" rounds. Cut 2 tablespoons butter into 6 equal portions. Place a butter piece on top of each biscuit. Spoon the remaining dough over the biscuits. Spread the dough slightly to make 6 biscuits about 3" round. The biscuits will be your shortcakes. Bake for 15 minutes or until the biscuits are golden brown.

Make the filling while the biscuits cook. In a sauce pan over medium heat, add 6 tablespoons butter. When the butter melts, add the ham. Stir frequently and cook until the ham browns or about 4 minutes. Stir in the all purpose flour, black pepper, Worcestershire sauce and chicken bouillon cube. Stir constantly and cook for 2 minutes. The mixture should begin to bubble. Keep stirring and add 3 1/2 cups milk. Stir until the sauce thickens and bubbles. Cook for 1 minute after the filling boils. Remove the pan from the heat and stir in the hard boiled eggs and parsley. Split the biscuits open and spoon the filling over the biscuits. Serve hot.

Easter Monday Dinner

This dish is a tradition in our family for Monday night dinner after Easter. My mother made it once a year and I continue to make it for my family. It uses up leftover hard boiled eggs and ham.

Makes 6 servings

2 cups diced cooked ham
4 tbs. unsalted butter
3 cups sliced zucchini
4 tbs. all purpose flour
1 tsp. dried dill
2 tsp. instant chicken bouillon granules
14 oz. can evaporated milk
1/2 cup water
6 hard boiled eggs, peeled and quartered

In a skillet over medium heat, add the butter. When the butter melts, add the ham. Stir frequently and cook until the ham browns or about 5 minutes. Remove the ham from the skillet and set aside.

Add the zucchini to the skillet. Stir frequently and place a lid on the skillet. Reduce the heat to low. Cook the zucchini about 15 minutes or until the zucchini are tender. Sprinkle the all purpose flour, dill and chicken bouillon over the zucchini. Stir until well combined.

Stir in the evaporated milk and water. Stir until well combined. Stir constantly and cook until the sauce thickens and bubbles. Add the ham and stir to combine. Place the egg quarters over the ham and heat only until the ham and eggs are warm.

Thanksgiving Leftover Stuffed Burgers

Makes 8 servings

2 1/2 cups leftover stuffing
2 eggs, beaten
3 lbs. ground beef
Salt to season meat
1 cup leftover whole cranberry sauce
2 tbs. vegetable oil
1 tbs. yellow prepared mustard
11 oz. jar beef gravy or leftover gravy
8 hoagie rolls, split, toasted and buttered

In a mixing bowl, add the stuffing and eggs. Preheat the oven to 400°. Divide the ground beef into 8 portions. Pat each portion into an 8" square. Sprinkle the ground beef with salt to taste. Place about 1/3 cup of the stuffing in the center of each square. Roll the ground beef up like a jelly roll. Place the patties on a baking sheet.

Add the cranberry sauce, mustard and vegetable oil to a blender. Blend until the mixture is well pureed. Brush the cranberry sauce over the burgers. Bake the burgers for 20-25 minutes or until the burgers are done and no longer pink. Brush the cranberry sauce on the burgers several times during the cooking process.

Heat the beef gravy in the microwave or on the stove top. Remove the burgers from the oven and place on hoagie rolls. Spoon the beef gravy over the top of the burgers to serve.

Ham Salad Spread

Makes 2 1/4 cups. This is a good use for leftover ham. Grind the ham in a food processor if desired.

2 cups cooked ground ham
1/2 cup finely chopped celery
1/4 cup sweet pickle relish
1/2 cup mayonnaise
1 tsp. prepared horseradish

Place all the ingredients in a mixing bowl. Stir until well combined. Chill until ready to use or at least 2 hours. Spread on bread for sandwiches or spread on crackers. The recipe can serve double duty as a meat dip for appetizers.

Stuffed Ham Steaks

Makes 4 servings

This is a great way to use up leftover ham, stuffing and cranberry sauce.

2 large leftover ham slices, about 1/2" thick
1 cup leftover stuffing
1 lb. can whole cranberry sauce

Preheat the oven to 350°. Place one ham slice in a baking dish. Spread the cranberry sauce over each ham slice. Spoon the stuffing over the ham slice in the pan. Place the remaining ham slice on top. Press the top ham slice down to mash together.

Bake for 40 minutes or until the ham and filling are hot. Remove the pan from the oven and serve.

Serve with a fruit salad and iced tea for a quick dinner.

Chapter Index

Stuffings & Dressings

Southern Cornbread Dressing, 45
Baked Fruit Dressing, 46
Sausage Cornbread Stuffing, 47
Sausage Bread Stuffing, 48
Raisin Walnut Stuffing, 49
Old Fashioned Potato Stuffing, 50
Oyster Stuffing, 51
Vegetable Stuffing, 52
Pumpernickel Stuffing, 52
Cranberry Pecan Stuffing, 53
Apple Walnut Sourdough Stuffing, 54
Pineapple Stuffing, 55
Herb Stuffing, 56
Mushroom Stuffing, 57
Sausage Apple Stuffing, 58
Parsley Stuffing, 59
Orange Stuffing, 60
Lemon Herb Stuffing, 61
Bacon and Herb Stuffing, 62
Brown Rice Stuffing, 63
Apricot Stuffing, 64
Wild Rice Stuffing, 65
Mock Wild Rice Dressing, 66
Rice and Corn Dressing, 67
Fruity Rice Stuffing, 68

Sauces, Glazes & Gravy

Maple Pecan Ham Glaze or Sauce, 70
Cranberry Glaze, 70
Baked Ham Pineapple Glaze, 71
Giblet Gravy, 72
Onion Mushroom Turkey Gravy, 73
Pan Drippings Gravy, 74
Easy and Quick Canned Soup Gravy, 75
Duck Gravy, 76
Garlic Oregano Meat Marinade, 76
Smoky Brisket Sauce, 77
Spicy Pork Dry Rub, 77
Beef Dry Rub, 78
Seafood Cajun Dry Rub, 78
Barbecue Sauce, 79
Wine Mushroom Butter, 80

Side Dishes

Baked Stuffed Yellow Squash, 82
Cheddar Squash Bake, 83
Fruit Filled Acorn Squash, 84
Candied Butternut Squash, 84
Mama's Squash Casserole, 85
Lemon Parsley Carrots, 85
Carrots Au Gratin, 86
Orange Baby Carrots, 86
Maple Apple Carrots, 87
Corn Custard Casserole, 87
Barbecue Corn, 88
Grilled Corn, 88
Easy Baked Beans, 89
Basil Tomatoes, 89
Marinated Tomatoes, 90
Tomato Onion Salad, 90
Grilled Tomatoes in Foil, 91
Lemon Green Beans, 91
Scalloped Green Beans, 92
Vegetable Casserole, 93
Sweet Caramelized Potatoes, 94
Marshmallow Whipped Sweet Potatoes, 94
Sweet Potato Balls, 95
Summer Garden Potato Salad, 96
Baby Barbecued Potatoes, 96
Mushroom Scalloped Potatoes, 97
Homemade Scalloped Potatoes, 98
Sour Cream Potato Salad, 99
Amaretto Sweet Potatoes, 100
Maple Syrup Sweet Potatoes, 101
Coconut Sweet Potato Bake, 102
Candied Sweet Potatoes, 102
Brussel Sprouts with Bacon, 103
Spinach Au Gratin, 103
Turnip Greens with Bacon, 104
Southern Cole Slaw, 105
English Pea Slaw, 105
Tangerine Rice, 106
Chili Bean Salad, 107
Garden Row Salad, 108
Potato Vegetable Salad, 109
Artichoke Salad, 110
Stardust Salad, 111
Summer Fruit Bowl, 112
Minted Melon Balls, 112

Grilled Cantaloupe Wedges, 113
Deviled Eggs, 113
Purple Hull Peas, 114

Breads

Sage Dinner Braid, 116
Onion Kuchen, 117
Cheese Loaf, 118
Ribbon Cheese Loaf, 119
Herb Cheese Pull Apart Rolls, 120
Perfect Sunday Dinner Rolls, 121
Onion Biscuits, 122
Super Fast Garlic Bread Sticks, 123
Salty No Yeast Bread Sticks, 124

Desserts: Pies, Cakes, Cookies & Candies

Brunch

Sausage Pie, 188
Apple Brunch Strata, 189
Overnight Veggie Sausage Strata, 190
Three Cheese Quiche, 191
Spinach Mushroom Breakfast Casserole, 192
Parmesan Omelet with Cheddar Sauce, 193
Pear Almond Quesadillas, 194
Apple Pancakes with Cider Sauce, 195
Island Pancakes, 196
Orange Yogurt Pancakes, 197
Southern Waffles, 198
Pecan Waffles, 199
Refrigerator Yeast Waffles or Pancakes, 200
Baked Orange French Toast, 201
Caramel Pecan Bubble Ring, 202
Apple Cinnamon Rolls, 203
Orange Bow Knots, 205
Cinnamon Muffin Bread, 206
Miniature Lemon Sugar Loaves, 206
Chess Squares Coffee Cake, 207
Blueberry Orange Bread, 208
Easy Sausage Mini Muffins, 209
Buttery Vanilla Breakfast Scones, 209
Blackberry Dumplings, 210
Puff Pancake with Summer Berries, 211
Blueberry Peach Breakfast Pudding, 212
Seafood Rice Salad, 213
Puffed Salad Bowl with Ham Salad, 214
Rotel Grits, 215
Pear Macaroon Salad, 215
Honey Fruit Salad, 216
Sweetened Grapes, 216
Banana Split Salad, 217
Cherry Pineapple Cups, 217
Cinnamon Honey Butter, 218

Beverages

Champagne Peach Punch, 220
Orange Mint Juleps, 220
Trader's Punch, 221
Cranberry Punch, 221
Tea Berry Sangria, 222
Red Roosters, 222
Whiskey Sour Punch, 223
Daiquiri Punch Bowl, 223
Orange Blossoms, 224
Orange and Strawberry Cream, 224
Blueberry Apple Juice Blast, 224
Melon Mango Juice, 225
Louisiana Cherry Bounce, 225

Leftovers

ABOUT THE AUTHOR

Lifelong southerner who lives in Bowling Green, KY. Priorities in life are God, family and pets. I love to cook, garden and feed most any stray animal that walks into my yard. I love old cookbooks and cookie jars. Huge NBA fan who loves to spend hours watching basketball games. Enjoy cooking for family and friends and hosting parties and reunions. Can't wait each year to build gingerbread houses for the kids.

Made in the USA
Columbia, SC
25 October 2020

23451285R00159